D0613385

The Investment Climate in Brazil, India, and South Africa

The Investment Climate in Brazil, India, and South Africa

A Comparison of Approaches for Sustaining Economic Growth in Emerging Economies

by
Qimiao Fan
José Guilherme Reis
Michael Jarvis
Andrew Beath
Kathrin Frauscher

WBI Learning Resource Series

 World Bank
Washington, D.C.

© 2008 The International Bank for Reconstruction and Development/The World Bank
1818 H Street, NW
Washington, DC 20433
Telephone: 202-473-1000
Internet: www.worldbank.org
E-mail: feedback@worldbank.org

All rights reserved
First printing November 2007

1 2 3 4 5 10 09 08 07

This volume is a product of the staff of the International Bank for Reconstruction and
Development/The World Bank. The findings, interpretations, and conclusions expressed in this
paper do not necessarily reflect the views of the Executive Directors of The World Bank or the
governments they represent.

The World Bank does not guarantee the accuracy of the data included in this work. The
boundaries, colors, denominations, and other information shown on any map in this work do not
imply any judgement on the part of The World Bank concerning the legal status of any territory
or the endorsement or acceptance of such boundaries.

Rights and Permissions
The material in this publication is copyrighted. Copying and/or transmitting portions or all of
this work without permission may be a violation of applicable law. The International Bank for
Reconstruction and Development/The World Bank encourages dissemination of its work and will
normally grant permission to reproduce portions of the work promptly.

For permission to photocopy or reprint any part of this work, please send a request with complete
information to the Copyright Clearance Center Inc., 222 Rosewood Drive, Danvers, MA 01923,
USA; telephone: 978-750-8400; fax: 978-750-4470; Internet: www.copyright.com.

All other queries on rights and licenses, including subsidiary rights, should be addressed to the
Office of the Publisher, The World Bank, 1818 H Street NW, Washington, DC 20433, USA; fax:
202-522-2422; e-mail: pubrights@worldbank.org.

Library of Congress Cataloging-in-Publication data has been applied for.

ISBN: 978-0-8213-7363-7
eISBN: 978-0-8213-7364-4
DOI: 10.1596/978-0-8213-7363-7

Cover and publication design: James E. Quigley
Cover photo: Photos.com

Contents

Boxes

Figures

Tables

Foreword

Few trends have captured the public imagination and the interest of economists and policy makers as the sustained rise of middle-income countries in recent years. These fast-growing economies are producing world-beating companies and creating new opportunities for their large populations.

Although none of these countries has followed a preordained path, each has provided its own valuable lessons of experience.

It was to share these experiences that business and government leaders met in Brasilia in September 2006 for the "1st Summit Meeting of the India-Brazil-South Africa Dialogue Forum (IBSA)." This volume is based on a comparative study of the investment climate in these three countries prepared by the World Bank Institute for presentation at the IBSA summit.

Development experience in recent decades suggests that a strong investment climate is central economic growth and poverty reduction. Key determinants of the investment climate include economic and political stability, rule of law, infrastructure, approaches to regulations and taxes, functioning of labor and finance markets, and broader features of governance, such as corruption. The World Bank group has long been a supporter of investment climate reform, recognizing the importance of shaping a business environment conducive to the successful start-up and operation of firms of all sizes in all sectors.

Facilitating the exchange of global and local knowledge and learning is an important part of the World Bank Institute's overall capacity development strategy. The Institute identifies countries' capacity needs and provides relevant products and services, including technical assistance, courses and seminars, cabinet-level retreats, and other activities that support the South-South exchange of knowledge. By drawing on the wealth of information captured in the World Bank's *Doing Business* indicators and enterprise surveys, this volume attempts to assess the factors that contribute to the creation of a robust investment climate and to share best practices and lessons learned from these three global players.

I believe this book will be a useful tool for policy makers in helping to foster an attractive investment climate—a solid platform for sustained economic success.

Rakesh Nangia
Acting Vice President
World Bank Institute

Acknowledgments

We would first like to thank the authors of individual World Bank investment climate assessments for Brazil, India, and South Africa for providing such rich sources for this publication. This work draws heavily on their findings, often using their analysis for detailing the situation in each of the countries.

We would also like to thank our colleagues whose advice and expertise greatly contributed to this publication's development, including Priya Basu, Simon C. Bell, John Briscoe, Michael Carter, George R. Clarke, Jacqui Coolidge, Inderbir Singh Dhingra, Shanthi Divakaran, W. Bernard Drum, Mark Andrew Dutz, Ruben Enikolopov, Leonardo Garrido, Alvaro Gonzales, Isabel Guerrero, James Habyarimana, Giuseppe Iarossi, Michael Ingram, David Kaplan, Vijaya Ramachandran, Ritva S. Reinekka, Jennifer Sara, Richard Stern, Yevgeniya Savchenko, Hong W. Tan, Marina Wes, L. Colin Xu, and Qinghua Zhao. In particular, we greatly appreciate the contributions of Mariam Dayoub to the content on Brazil. Finally, we would like to thank John Didier, James Quigley, Elizabeth Forsyth, and Alexis Sampson for their support in the editing and layout of this book and Alexander Fleming for his overall direction of the project.

Abbreviations

ASGISA	Accelerated and Shared Growth Initiative for South Africa
BPO	Business process outsourcing
CIBIL	Credit Information Bureau of India Limited
Confins	Social financial contributions (Contribuição Financeira Social)
CSLL	Social contributions on net profits (Contribuição Social sobre o Lucro Líquido)
GDP	Gross domestic product
IBSA	India, Brazil, and South Africa Dialogue Forum
ICA	Investment Climate Assessment
ICMS	State sales tax (Imposto de Circulação de Mercadorias e Serviços)
ICS	Investment Climate Survey
ICT	Information and communications technology
IMF	International Monetary Fund
INSS	Federal taxes, including social security
IPI	Tax on manufactured goods (Imposto sobre Produtos Industrializados)
IRPJ	Business federal tax responsibilities (Imposto de Renda Pessoa Jurídica)
ISS	Municipal tax on services (Imposto sobre Serviços)
ITES	Information technology enabling services
IT	Information technology
MSE	Micro and small enterprise
NASSCOM	National Association of Software and Services Companies (India)
OECD	Organisation for Economic Co-operation and Development
PAN	Permanent account number

P<small>ASEP</small>	Asset-Building Program for Public Workers (Programa de Formação do Patrimônio do Servidor Público)
PIS	Social Integration Program (Programa de Integração Social)
SADC	Southern African Development Community
SARFAESI	Securitization and Reconstruction of Financial Assets and Enforcement of Security Interest Act
SARS	South African Revenue Service
SME	Small and medium-size enterprise
STC	Secondary tax on corporations
STPI	Software Technology Parks of India
TFP	Total factor productivity

1

Introduction

The central challenge in reaping greater benefits from globalization lies in improving the investment climate—that is, in providing sound regulation of industry, including the promotion of competition; in overcoming bureaucratic delay and inefficiency; in fighting corruption; and in improving the quality of infrastructure. While the investment climate is clearly important for large, formal sector firms, it is just as important—if not more so—for small and medium enterprises (SMEs), the informal sector, agricultural productivity, and the generation of off-farm employment. For these reasons, the investment climate itself is a key issue for poverty reduction. [Stern 2001]

Broad-based economic growth is the most important driver of poverty reduction and improved living standards. Such growth, however, only occurs when firms and entrepreneurs of all types are given appropriate incentives to invest productively in human and physical capacity and to heighten the productivity of factor inputs. A strong investment climate is a platform for economic success.

This central lesson of economics, although simple, is ill-learned. Throughout the world, misguided regulations and inadequate infrastructure burden firms with unnecessary costs, considerable uncertainty and risk, and unjustified barriers to competition. As a result, many segments of the population are hindered from contributing productively to the economy and from sharing in the considerable opportunities opened up by broad-based economic growth. Changing this situation for the better is only possible through reform of the investment climate.

This book is based on a comparative study, "The Investment Climate in Brazil, India, South Africa," that was prepared for the first summit of the India, Brazil, and South Africa Dialogue Forum (IBSA), which was held in Brasilia,

Brazil, in September 2006 (Beath 2006). During the forum, Brazilian President Luiz Inacio Lula da Silva, Indian Prime Minister Manmohan Singh, and South African President Thabo Mbeki highlighted not only the growing trade relations and the enhanced cooperation among their countries with regard to global public goods but also the growing importance of South-South sharing of experiences in institutional development, planning, regulation, and financing.

With this book, we seek to contribute to this sharing of knowledge between Brazil, India, and South Africa, three of the largest emerging economies today. By assessing and comparing the investment climate in each, we seek to profile concrete steps that countries can take to improve the business environment. We focus particularly on identifying the commonalities and differences both within and among the three countries and attempt to highlight examples where policy makers will be able to drawn on the lessons from their own reform experiences and those of their counterparts in other core emerging markets. Specifically, we consider the following questions:

- What are the most binding constraints for enterprises in Brazil, India, and South Africa?
- What can Brazil, India, South Africa, and other emerging economies learn from one another in reforming the investment climate?
- What can the three countries learn from in-country variations in the investment climate?
- What tools might assist policy makers in pinpointing priority reforms of the investment climate?

Our analysis demonstrates that the business constraints differ among the three countries, particularly with regard to the leading reform priority, but that there are also issues of shared concern. For example, firms in all three countries list tax rates among their top five constraints to doing business. Often two of these emerging economies have identified the same problem issues. Macroeconomic instability is the second most frequently cited concern in Brazil and South Africa. In the 2003 surveys both Indian and Brazilian firms cited policy uncertainty among their most pressing constraints.

These areas of commonality and difference among the investment climates of Brazil, India, and South Africa, and especially some of the recent investment climate reforms, provide opportunities for mutual intercountry benchmarking and learning. South Africa's experience with tax reforms could be instructive for Brazil, while Brazil's experience with reforming bankruptcy procedures could be of real interest to India. In a number of areas, such as skilled labor policies, India has much knowledge to impart to Brazil and South Africa. The three countries can also learn from their own experiences. In Brazil and India, in particular, substantial differences exist between regions regarding different aspects of the investment climate. In many cases, substantial improvements in the overall investment climate could be achieved if all of the states within a country would adopt reforms that have worked particularly well in specific parts of the country.

The benchmarking within and among countries can be a starting point for dialogue between the government and private sector on priorities for reform and help to encourage the sharing of best practices among Brazil, India, South Africa, and other emerging economies. The challenge is to prioritize areas for reform and build momentum to sustain and broaden existing restructuring efforts. The analysis and case studies presented in this book are intended to assist policy makers in maintaining the momentum for continued strengthening of the investment climate.

The book is organized as follows. Chapter 2 provides a brief overview of the investment climate in each of the three countries, highlighting the key constraints identified by the national business communities, and explains the underlying concepts of the investment climate assessments and Doing Business indicators. Chapter 3 examines the macroeconomic performance of Brazil, India, and South Africa and shows how the three countries perform with regard to taxation and foreign trade and exchange. Chapter 4 reviews key microeconomic regulations, such as rules regarding the entry and exit of firms and labor regulations, and assesses the enforcement of contracts and regulations. Chapter 5 studies the set of services, factors, and conditions that firms require when establishing operations and engaging in production and exchange, including access to finance, physical infrastructure, cost and availability of labor, and security. Chapter 6 considers methods to assess the impact of potential reforms that could be undertaken at the national level to improve the investment climate and provides sample calculations. Chapter 7 offers guidance on how to manage investment climate reforms by showcasing best-practice examples from recent reforms in Brazil, India, and South Africa. A final chapter concludes.

2

Assessing the Investment Climate of Brazil, India, and South Africa

Variations in investment climate have recently received close attention from policy makers, in particular regarding the explanation for differences in economic growth across locations and countries. A good investment climate fosters productive private investment and economic growth by creating opportunities for the private sector to invest, create jobs, and lay the foundations for long-term business success (World Bank 2005c).

The investment climate is defined as the institutional, policy, and regulatory environment in which firms operate.[1] Key determinants of the investment climate include economic and political stability, rule of law, infrastructure, approaches to regulations and taxes, functioning of labor and finance markets, and broader features of governance, such as corruption (World Bank 2005c). This book uses data from the World Bank investment climate surveys, which provide the basis for the investment climate assessments, as well as the World Bank Doing Business reports in order to analyze and compare the investment climate of Brazil, India, and South Africa (see appendix A for more information on the investment climate concept, means of assessment, and data sources).

Based on these data sources, it is clear that *the investment climate in Brazil, India, and South Africa shows substantial scope for improvement* (see table 2.1). The 2007 Doing Business report ranks Brazil and India 121st and 134th, respectively, out of 175 countries surveyed according to the extent to which regulations impede the operation of a hypothetical firm (World Bank 2007b). South Africa performs better, ranking 29th on the list, although it scores below

---

1. This definition arises from Dollar, Hallward-Driemeier, and Mengistae (2005). The World Bank's 2005 World Development Report defines the investment climate as a set of location-specific factors shaping the opportunities and incentives for firms to invest productively, create jobs, and expand (World Bank 2005c).

Table 2.1
Select Economies Ranked According to the Ease of Doing Business

Economy	Rank	Economy	Rank	Economy	Rank	Economy	Rank
Singapore	1	Jamaica	50	China	93	**India**	**134**
Hong Kong, China	5	Maldives	53	Russia	96	Indonesia	135
Thailand	18	Uruguay	64	Nepal	100	Mozambique	140
Korea, Rep. of	23	Nicaragua	67	Argentina	101	Iraq	145
Malaysia	25	Pakistan	74	Nigeria	108	Senegal	146
Chile	28	Colombia	79	Greece	109	Zimbabwe	153
South Africa	**29**	Italy	82	Paraguay	112	Venezuela	164
Mauritius	32	Kenya	83	Iran, Islamic Rep. of	119	Sierra Leone	168
Armenia	34	Bangladesh	88	**Brazil**	**121**	Timor-Leste	174
Namibia	42	Sri Lanka	89	Philippines	126	Congo, D.R.	175

Source: World Bank (2006a).

business centers in a number of other emerging economies, such as Chile, Malaysia, and Thailand.[2]

A comparison of the three economies reveals *substantial differences in their investment climate conditions*, particularly regarding which facets serve as the most binding constraints for enterprises (see table 2.2). The highest ranked constraint differs for each country, and each has unique constraints among its top five.

However, there are also common *areas of concern*. Most notably, managers in all three countries list tax rates as among their top five concerns. Medium-size firms operating in Rio de Janeiro face total tax rates that can exceed gross profits, while those in São Paulo must spend 2,600 hours a year preparing, filing, and paying taxes, also the highest in the world.[3] Although India and South

---

2. In Brazil a majority of firms rank the top issues as a severe or extremely severe obstacle to growth; for example, 84 percent respond that tax rates are a severe obstacle. However, for South Africa and India, no one issue is ranked as a severe obstacle by a majority of respondents. The first-ranked constraints in South Africa (skills) and India (corruption) are considered as such by only 37 and 35 percent of the firms surveyed, respectively. The responses from Brazil were compared with those of 60 countries, and it was found that Brazil had the second higher level of perceived obstacles (Mozambique had the highest). The reason why remains unclear. There appears to be no systematic bias in the data collection. The survey was carried out in the whole country, by different teams, and the numbers do not differ much by state or region. One possible explanation could be the effect of low economic growth on business expectations. The World Bank explored different econometric specifications to correct the perceptions in different countries for the economic cycle, with no significant result. However, the economic, cultural, and political context could have played a role given that the ICS was carried out in 2003, when Brazil's economy was facing recession, having experienced economic turmoil the year before and following five years of low economic growth.

3. The 2006 Doing Business data (World Bank 2006a) suggests a tax rate that goes above 200 percent as a share of corporate profits as consumption taxes are included in the calculation, considering a firm with a 20 percent profit margin and value of sales equal to 120 percent of value of inputs. Since consumption taxes are high (above the firm's profit margin), the firm can end up paying more tax than its corporate profits. In the 2007 report (World Bank 2007b), this problem was corrected and consumption taxes were not included. As a result, the tax rate for

Table 2.2

Top Five Business Constraints Identified by Managers

Brazil		India		South Africa	
Constraint	*Percent*	*Constraint*	*Percent*	*Constraint*	*Percent*
Tax rates	84	Corruption	37	Skills	35
Macroeconomic instability	83	Electricity	29	Macroeconomic instability	34
Policy uncertainty	76	Tax rates	28	Labor regulations	33
Cost of finance	75	Tax administration	27	Crime	29
Tax administration	66	Policy uncertainty	21	Tax rates	19

Source: World Bank, ICS for Brazil (2003), India (2003), and South Africa (2004).
Note: Figures represent the share of respondents citing the characteristic as a "major" or "very severe" obstacle "for the operation and growth of your business." Results from the 2003 ICS in India are included to allow for greater comparability with the data from Brazil and South Africa for a similar time period. However, 2006 ICS data list the top five business constraints in India as electricity (36 percent), tax rates (35 percent), corruption (28 percent), tax administration (27 percent), and cost and access to finance (16 percent).

Africa generally have more efficient tax systems than Brazil, there is room for improvement. Despite relatively moderate tax levels, South African firms must spend an inordinate amount of time—some 350 hours a year—filing 23 annual payments. Indian firms must submit 1.5 times more tax payments than their counterparts in other South Asian business centers.

Often two of these leading emerging economies share the same concern regarding the investment climate. Macroeconomic instability is the second most frequently cited concern in Brazil and South Africa, which is not surprising given the pronounced volatility of both the real and the rand. Although South Africa lacks the history of hyperinflation that has haunted the Brazilian macroeconomy, both countries have recently experienced relatively high and volatile levels of inflation, which may be reflected in the responses.[4] In both of these regards, Brazil and South Africa have something to learn from India, which has had remarkable success in maintaining stable price levels over the past five years. A concern related to macroeconomic stability is policy uncertainty, which is frequently cited by managers in both Brazil and India, underscoring the fear that political currents will threaten economic reform.

Lending rates in Brazil are extremely high, and the cost of finance is identified as a problem by three-quarters of Brazilian firms. Indian firms, particularly

---

Brazil was 71.7 percent of corporate profits. Regarding tax administration, the figure of 2,600 hours to fill out tax forms reflects the fact that the Brazilian legislation is complicated, complex and disperse at all government levels. In addition, there are frequent changes to the taxation system. Therefore, a person filling out corporate tax forms should read the tax legislation at the federal, state, and municipal level as well as the legislative alterations. This would take a long time, giving rise to the figure of 2,600 hours that reflects the estimated "reading" preparation process.

4. Moreover, in the case of Brazil, since the ICS was carried out in 2003, the responses might have reflected private sector reactions to a recent period of high volatility of interest and exchange rates, a peak in inflation, and low output growth.

smaller ones, also have a difficult time getting access to credit (World Bank 2004). In South Africa, access to and the cost of credit are lesser concerns (World Bank 2007a).

Indian managers are primarily concerned about issues of infrastructure provision and corruption. Results from the 2006 Investment Climate Survey (ICS) in India suggest that electricity supply is now the biggest constraint for Indian firms, cited by 36 percent of respondents, up from 29 percent in the 2003 survey.[5] Generally, the status of infrastructure in India, which includes the state of power supply, telecommunication services, transport, and water, is far from satisfactory, as revealed by India's competitiveness rankings (World Bank 2004). While infrastructure is not a leading concern in South Africa, this issue does resonate with many firms in Brazil. Surveys suggest that the quality of the power supply is a problem for firms in Brazil, particularly in the northern regions. (For further detail, see the section on investment climate and firm location in chapter 5.)

Similarly, corruption is a key concern, not just in India, but also in Brazil, where more than half of respondents in the enterprise surveys list corruption as a major constraint on their business. Once again, South Africa is an exception, with surveys indicating that South African firms are not particularly concerned about issues of graft.

Among South African businesses, the highest ranked concern is the availability and cost of skilled workers, although the rigidity of labor regulations and crime are not far behind. Both of these latter two issues are also of concern to half of Brazilian managers (World Bank 2007c).

The results of the Doing Business study point to several other specific issues that affect the economic performance of the three countries (see table 2.3). In both Brazil and India, the judiciary has a poor relationship with business. The problem in Brazil is primarily with procedures for bankruptcy, which in turn create difficulties for Brazilian firms in accessing finance. India, meanwhile, has severe problems with the enforcement of contracts, although bankruptcy procedures are also inefficient (World Bank 2004). Regulation imposes an unusual administrative and financial burden on enterprises in both Brazil and India and, to a lesser extent, in South Africa. The rigidity of labor regulation in Brazil is particularly constraining. India also scores poorly in terms of the burden of licensing and permit requirements for ongoing business operations and the time, cost, and administrative procedures required to import or export goods.[6] Such regulations raise the cost of doing business, fostering a high level of informality,

---

5. The survey results have not yet been formally released, but the data and summary are available online at http://www.enterprisesurveys.org/.

6. The India investment climate assessment for 2004 reports that substantial progress has been made in some of these indicators (World Bank 2004). For instance, the number of factory inspections per year fell from 11.7 in 2000 to 7.4 in 2003, and the average number of days spent clearing industrial imports through customs also fell from 10.3 in 2000 to 7.3 in 2003.

Table 2.3
Ease of Doing Business in São Paulo, Johannesburg, and Mumbai

Indicator	São Paulo	Johannesburg	Mumbai
Starting a business	115	57	88
Dealing with licenses	139	45	155
Employing workers	99	87	112
Registering property	124	69	110
Getting credit	83	33	65
Protecting investors	60	9	33
Paying taxes	151	74	158
Trading across borders	53	67	139
Enforcing contracts	120	43	173
Closing a business	135	65	133

Source: World Bank (2006a, 2007c, 2007d).

which in turn deprives both federal and state governments of tax revenue and makes it more difficult for firms to access credit markets and utility services.[7] On the plus side, Brazil, India, and South Africa, in particular, do relatively well in protecting minority investors from the misuse of corporate assets.

An assessment of differences and commonalities among the investment climates in Brazil, India, and South Africa suggests that there is *substantial scope for learning among the three countries*. In a number of areas, India has much to impart to Brazil and South Africa. Skilled labor is both more readily available and relatively inexpensive in India than in Brazil and South Africa. The stability of India's exchange rate contrasts with the volatility of exchange rates in Brazil and South Africa, which provides another area for mutual learning and assistance. South Africa's experience with tax reforms could be instructive for Brazil, where taxation is extremely burdensome, both administratively and financially, a fact that stems from the rigid revenue needs of central and state governments. Similarly, Brazil and India could learn much from South Africa in improving public administration, improving access to finance, upgrading the quality of physical infrastructure, and reducing the burden of regulation governing market entry and exit and employment.

In support of cross-border sharing of knowledge and learning, it is useful to be able to assess the value of potential reforms in determining priorities. The World Bank has developed the Doing Business Ranking Simulator, a tool for

---

7. According to World Bank (2007c), informality accounted for approximately 42 percent of Brazil's output in 2002–03; the comparable figures are 16 percent for China, 26 percent for India, and 33 percent for Mexico. Moreover, if Brazil would improve its Doing Business indicators to the level of the top 30 countries, the share of GDP accounted for by informal activity would fall an estimated 9 percentage points.

simulating some of the potential gains that could be realized by making changes in specific areas.[8] For instance, noting that tax rates are among the top five constraints identified by the private sector in Brazil and India, but not a major concern in South Africa, we can simulate the impact on each country's Doing Business ranking if Brazil and India were to reduce the tax burden to South Africa's level. If Brazil would reduce its total tax rate (of profit) from 71.7 percent to the South African rate of 38.3 percent, it would improve its ease of Doing Business ranking from 121st to 114th. If India did the same, reducing the total rate from 81.1 to 38.3 percent, the country would improve nine places in the rankings. Alternatively, turning to another leading constraint faced by Indian business—tax administration—if India were to improve the ease of paying taxes from the 0.77 percentile to South Africa's 0.45 percentile in the 2007 Doing Business data, India would leap 15 places from 134 to 119 in the Doing Business simulated rankings. Similarly, turning to another leading constraint identified by Brazilian managers—the cost of finance—if the country were able to improve the ease of obtaining credit to South Africa's level of 0.27 from Brazil's current 0.57 percentile, it would leap in the Doing Business rankings from 121 to 109. Although these simulations have to be interpreted while paying close attention to their underlying assumptions,[9] they can help to reveal areas of reform where Brazil, India, and South Africa could improve their performance by learning from one another.[10]

Given the large size of Brazil and India and the authority afforded states, there are *significant differences within each country in the quality of the investment climate* (see tables 2.4 and 2.5).[11] World Bank (2007c) identifies a positive correlation between the ease of doing business in a state and the level of income. In Brazil the best performer, the Federal District, is also the wealthiest, while the worst performer, Ceará, is the second poorest state among the 13 surveyed. Nevertheless, there are exceptions. The poorest state, Maranhão, ranks

---

8.   The simulator can be accessed via http://www.doingbusiness.org/.

9.   Two important issues should be kept in mind when using these simulations. First, all calculations assume that the data for all other countries remain constant—that is, one country improves, and the rest remain unchanged. Second, assessing the impact of a reform in the Doing Business indicators may not be straightforward, meaning that reforms may not always have real-life impact because of many other factors not accounted for in the data.

10. Unfortunately the major constraints identified by South African business, such as availability of skilled labor and crime, are not so easily tracked by Doing Business indicators. However, if South Africa were to improve the "difficulty of hiring" index from its current ranking of 44 to India's ranking of 33, it would see a percentile improvement in its overall Doing Business ranking, although not an improvement sufficient to improve its ranking beyond the 29th place in the 2007 overall country rankings.

11. In Brazil, opening a business in the state of Minas Gerais takes only 19 days, compared to 152 days in São Paulo. By way of comparison, the difference between the best- and worst-performing state in Mexico is only twofold. Minas Gerais is in the top 30 worldwide in terms of the time it takes to start a business, whereas São Paulo ranks 149th out of 155.

Table 2.4
Ease of Doing Business in Brazilian States

State	Ranking
Federal District	1
Amazonas	2
Minas Gerais	3
Rondônia	4
Maranhão	5
Rio Grande do Sul	6
Mato Grosso do Sul	7
Rio de Janeiro	8
Santa Catarina	9
Bahia	10
São Paulo	11
Mato Grosso	12
Ceará	13

Source: World Bank (2007c).

Table 2.5
Ease of Doing Business in Indian Cities

City and state	Ranking
Bangalore, Karnataka	1
Jaipur, Rajasthan	2
Lucknow, Uttar Pradesh	3
Chandigarh, Punjab	4
Hyderabad, Andhra Pradesh	5
Bhubaneshwar, Orissa	6
Mumbai, Maharashtra	7
Chennai, Tamil Nadu	8
Kolkata, West Bengal	9

Source: World Bank (2007d).

5th out of 13 as a result of recent reforms to streamline the process for starting a business.[12]

In India, the Doing Business team found that, of nine cities, Bangalore is the easiest in which to start and operate a business, while Kolkata is the most

---

12. World Bank (2007c) reports, "Maranhão also introduced reforms to facilitate business start-ups. Information on new applications is now shared between the board of trade, the state tax authority, and the municipality, which evaluate and provide preliminary approvals. This reduces the risk of businesses starting the process of formalization at the board of trade, but not completing it with other agencies. Once the company is cleared for approval, the start-up process is faster."

Table 2.6

Top Five Business Constraints Identified by Managers in Four South African Regions

Gauteng		KwaZulu-Natal		Western Cape		Eastern Cape	
Constraint	*Percent*	*Constraint*	*Percent*	*Constraint*	*Percent*	*Constraint*	*Percent*
Worker skills	37	Worker skills	44	Macroeconomic instability	44	Macroeconomic instability	36
Labor regulations	32	Macroeconomic instability	44	Labor regulations	39	Trade regulation	31
Crime	31	Crime	41	Worker skills	30	Worker skills	19
Macroeconomic instability	28	Labor regulations	33	Crime	23	Cost of finance	19
Corruption	19	Tax rates	33	Policy uncertainty	22	Labor regulations	17

Source: World Bank ICS for South Africa (2004).
Note: Percentages represent the share of respondents citing characteristic as a "major" or "very severe" obstacle "for the operation and growth of your business."

difficult (World Bank 2007d). A surprising finding is that the relatively prosperous cities of Mumbai and Chennai rank 7th and 8th, well behind cities such as Jaipur and Lucknow. This evidence is contradicted somewhat, however, by data collected through the investment climate survey, which asked managers to identify the states they think have a better or worse investment climate than the state in which they were based at the time of the survey. In that analysis, Maharashtra comes out on top, with Uttar Pradesh, West Bengal, and Kerala scoring poorly. Results from the investment climate survey indicate that small- and medium-size enterprises receive factory inspections twice as frequently in the states assessed as having a poor investment climate as in those assessed as having a good climate. "Good-climate" states also have cheaper and more reliable power supplies, and for small- and medium-size enterprises in poor-climate states, the cost of generating power on their own is about twice as high as the price of purchasing power from the public grid.

Unlike Brazil and India, there are no data in the Doing Business indicators on variations within South Africa. However, the business constraints identified by the investment climate assessment do vary to some extent across provinces (see table 2.6). For instance, firms are more concerned about trade regulation in the Eastern Cape than in the other three provinces (31 versus 18 percent) and much less concerned about labor regulation (17 versus 35 percent), worker skills (19 versus 37 percent), and crime (6 versus 32 percent).

3

Macroeconomic and Trade Policy

When macroeconomic policy goes wrong, few firms are able to escape its effects. Rampant rates of inflation arbitrarily redistribute income across the economy and create enormous difficulties for firms wishing to operate with any semblance of normality (see figure 3.1). Volatile or misvalued exchange rates similarly generate costs for all those engaged regularly in international trade, either directly through arbitrary revaluations of their international competitiveness or

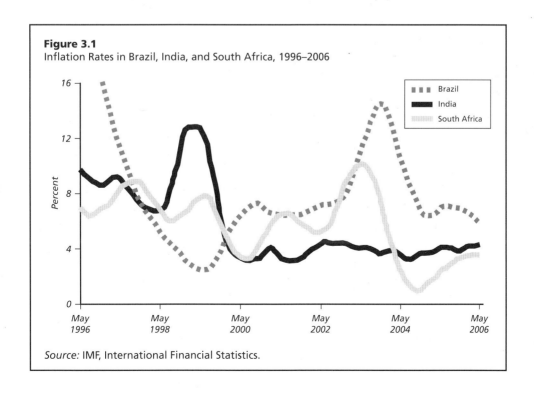

Figure 3.1
Inflation Rates in Brazil, India, and South Africa, 1996–2006

Source: IMF, International Financial Statistics.

indirectly through the costs of hedging. Poorly managed policies for public finance, meanwhile, inevitably lead to ineffective and costly taxation policies, which provide firms with an unwelcome choice between engaging in risky evasion or losing a substantial proportion of their profits. In this chapter, we examine and contrast the macroeconomic history and policies of Brazil, India, and South Africa, going beyond those identified as the leading constraints in the national surveys. We begin with an overview of recent growth and inflation, followed by taxation, and conclude with an overview of policies toward the external sector.

Macroeconomic Performance

Over recent decades, developing countries as a whole have grown quickly relative to historical trends. There has, however, been substantial diversity across countries, and the comparative experiences of Brazil, India, and South Africa demonstrate this diversity well. Brazil, for instance, rapidly achieved middle-income status, with dramatically high rates of economic growth in the late 1960s and early 1970s. Since then, however, it has experienced extreme macroeconomic volatility and, in recent years, recorded low rates of economic growth. India, in contrast, has a relatively low level of per capita income and, for much of the late twentieth century, experienced disappointing growth. Since the early 1980s, however, per capita growth has surged to robustly high levels. South Africa's growth historically has been much less volatile than Brazil's, although, like Brazil, South Africa has recorded negligible rates of growth in real per capita GDP in recent decades.

Brazil

Over the past 25 years, economic growth in Brazil has demonstrated substantial volatility around a relatively low mean (see figure 3.2). In the wake of chronic inflation that consumed much of the 1980s and early 1990s, the Brazilian economy is tentatively but steadily finding its way to macroeconomic stability. Throughout the early 2000s, inflation has remained at historically moderate rates. Interest rates have fallen, although they are higher in Brazil than in other countries. Unfortunately, the recent period of stabilization has not propelled rapid economic growth. Between 1979 and 2005, real per capita GDP grew only US$510 (in constant 2000 U.S. dollars).

Brazil has some of the highest levels of economic inequality in the world, a fact that is reflected in substantial disparities among regions in per capita income and economic growth (see figure 3.3). Brazil's richest area, the Federal

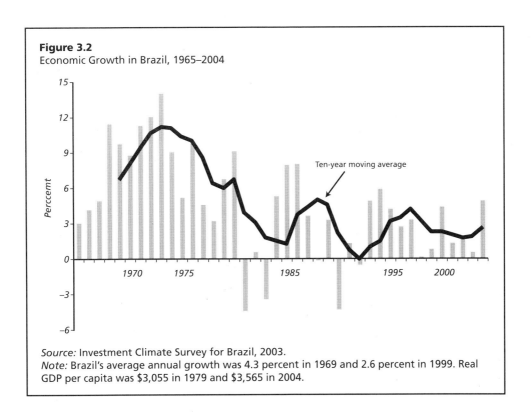

Figure 3.2
Economic Growth in Brazil, 1965–2004

Source: Investment Climate Survey for Brazil, 2003.
Note: Brazil's average annual growth was 4.3 percent in 1969 and 2.6 percent in 1999. Real GDP per capita was $3,055 in 1979 and $3,565 in 2004.

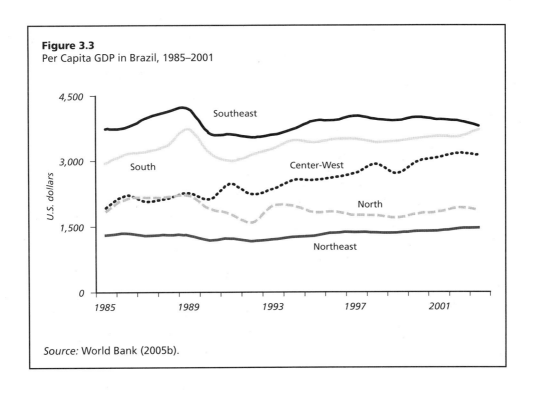

Figure 3.3
Per Capita GDP in Brazil, 1985–2001

Source: World Bank (2005b).

District, has a per capita income that is some six times greater than that of the poorest state, Maranhão. The southeastern region, which includes the states of Espírito Santo, Minas Gerais, Rio de Janeiro, and São Paulo, is the most prosperous in the country, although the economy of the center-west region, which encompasses the Federal District, has grown much faster than that of other regions over the past two decades. The volatility of growth rates across Brazilian states is extremely high: between 1986 and 2004 the standard deviation of GDP growth rates for Brazilian states was more than six times the mean.

India

In the early 1990s, the Indian economy broke from a history of disappointing economic performance and experienced rapid increases in GDP (see figure 3.4). Between 1994 and 1997, strong private investment spurred economic growth to levels in excess of 7 percent. Although growth lagged somewhat in the years thereafter, the economy grew 8.6 percent in 2003 (see figure 3.5). In total, between 1999 and 2004, the Indian economy grew an average of 5.7 percent annually. During this period, inflation remained at remarkably low levels, and the Indian government experienced considerable success in ensuring a relatively stable exchange rate and low rates of interest (World Bank 2004). Over the past

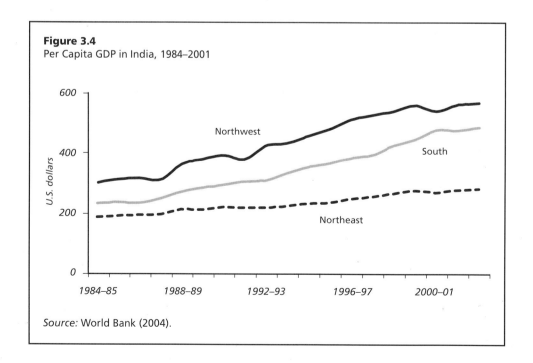

Figure 3.4
Per Capita GDP in India, 1984–2001

Source: World Bank (2004).

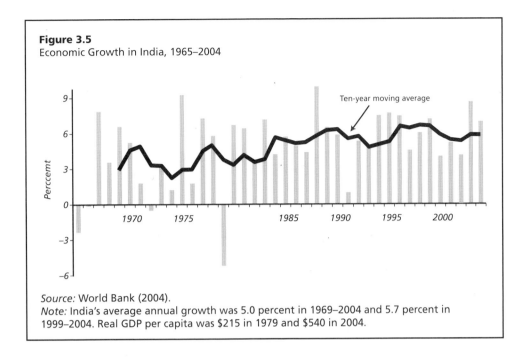

Figure 3.5
Economic Growth in India, 1965–2004

Source: World Bank (2004).
Note: India's average annual growth was 5.0 percent in 1969–2004 and 5.7 percent in 1999–2004. Real GDP per capita was $215 in 1979 and $540 in 2004.

three years, the growth performance has been stellar, with GDP growth in excess of 9 percent annually.

Despite the recent successes in spurring economic growth, per capita income in India was only US$815 in 2006–07 (per capita gross national income, Atlas method), even though it has nearly doubled since 2001–02. There are substantial (and, according to some indicators, increasing) regional disparities in income, and much of India's recent growth has been concentrated away from the poorer areas in the west and center of the subcontinent. Per capita income in Maharashtra is triple that in Bihar, and the rapid growth rates of prosperous states in the far north and south have quickly outstripped the negligible improvements of poorer states such as Madhya Pradesh, Orissa, and Rajasthan.

South Africa

Since the transition to democracy, South Africa's macroeconomic performance has been solid, but not spectacular (see figure 3.6). Between 1995 and 2004, annual GDP growth averaged about 3.4 percent. Prior to 1994, economic growth was extremely volatile, but since then it has stabilized. In this respect, South Africa appears locked onto a path of sustained but moderate growth. As South Africa's population has been increasing, per capita growth has been slower than total growth, averaging just 1.3 percent in the 10 years up to 2004. However, most recent economic performance has been strong. Government figures show

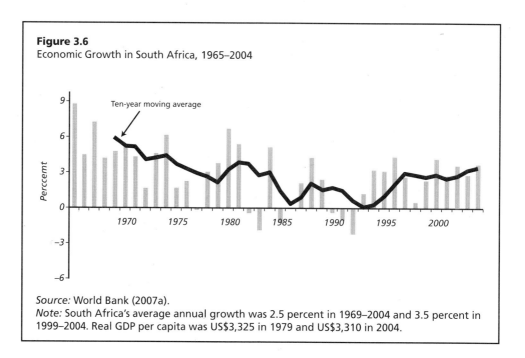

Figure 3.6
Economic Growth in South Africa, 1965–2004

Source: World Bank (2007a).
Note: South Africa's average annual growth was 2.5 percent in 1969–2004 and 3.5 percent in 1999–2004. Real GDP per capita was US$3,325 in 1979 and US$3,310 in 2004.

that South Africa's GDP grew 4.9 percent in 2006, with growth now projected to average about 5 percent a year over the period 2007–09.[1]

Taxation

There is no country where businesses do not complain about taxes. Yet taxes serve an essential purpose in providing funding for public goods such as education, health, the judicial system, infrastructure, and defense. Nevertheless, many governments have, over the years, been guilty of implementing tax policies that are both counterproductive for raising revenue and costly for economic growth. Among the three countries, the administrative and financial burden of taxation is most serious in Brazil (see table 3.1). In contrast, the burden of taxation on firms in India and South Africa is relatively in line with international norms, although India could lessen the number of tax payments made by firms, and South Africa could reduce the complexity of its system.

The Brazilian tax system is among the most complex and burdensome anywhere in the world. In 2005 the tax burden in Brazil reached 37.4 percent of GDP. A disproportionate amount is raised through taxes on business.[2] Ac-

---

1.   See http://www.southafrica.info/doing_business/economy/fiscal_policies/budget2007-fiscal.htm.

2   The high burden of taxation in Brazil is a relatively recent phenomenon, owing to the growth of the public sector during the 1990s and the absence of other means by which to reach fiscal balance.

Table 3.1
Administrative and Financial Burden of Taxes

City and region	Number of payments made a year	Time (hours spent)	Total tax payable (as a percent of gross profit)
São Paulo	23	2,600	147.9
Latin America	48	529	52.8
Mumbai	59	264	43.2
South Asia	26	332	35.3
Johannesburg	32	350	43.8
Sub-Saharan Africa	41	394	58.1
OECD	16	197	45.4

Source: World Bank (2006a).

countants estimate that it would consume a full 325 working days to comply with all tax requirements. In addition, Brazilian firms must cope with frequent changes in tax rates and rules, an onerous process of appeals, and extremely severe penalties for underpayment. Furthermore, the high level of financial taxation has added to the problem of wide spreads on interest rates, which in turn has increased the credit costs for firms. For this reason, Brazilian firms consider the level of taxation to be the most serious problem inhibiting their growth, with more than 80 percent of respondents citing taxation as a severe or extremely severe obstacle.

However, the government has enacted positive reform measures, such as the SIMPLES legislation, that simplify tax procedures for smaller enterprises (see the case study in chapter 7). In addition, firms operating in the north of the country generally see tax administration as less of an obstacle to business expansion than their counterparts in the southeast. The Doing Business team found that filing taxes is less complicated in the states of Bahia, Rondônia, and Mato Grosso do Sul and is most difficult in Mato Grosso, São Paulo, and Minas Gerais.

In India, recent reforms have attempted to simplify tax registration procedures, although the administrative and financial burden of tax payments remains high by international standards. Although Indian firms spend less time filing taxes than their South Asian counterparts, some 264 hours a year, the cumbersome tax regime requires 59 separate payments. Even more significant, the financial burden of the tax regime is extremely high by international standards, consuming some 81 percent of Indian firms' profits, compared with a regional average of just 45 percent. Accordingly, Indian firms cite both tax rates and tax administration among the top five most serious obstacles to doing business.[3]

---

3. This is true in both the 2003 and the 2006 ICS, although in 2006 only 28 percent of respondents rated tax rates as a major concern compared to 35 percent in 2003. The percentage rating

Small firms are even more likely to complain about the burden of taxation. Recent policy changes, particularly the adoption of a value added tax across most of the country in April 2006, should lessen such concerns somewhat. However, there is an urgent need to consolidate the sales and value added taxes collected at various levels of government and thereby to eliminate the hassle, both for firms and for bureaucracies, of having separate government agencies collect different taxes on the same tax base.

The administrative and financial burden of taxation for firms in South Africa is similar to that of India and considerably less than that faced by firms in other African countries. Corporate taxes have recently been reduced, and this has contributed to the relative satisfaction expressed by South African firms with their tax burden (World Bank 2007a).[4] Of particular interest is the substantial increase in the amount of revenue collected by the South African government through taxation, even as tax rates have fallen. From a base of 100 in 1995, revenue derived from taxes on companies doubled to 200.8 in 2000–01 and then more than doubled to 410.9 in 2003. The robust growth in tax revenues is a consequence of higher company profitability, improved enforcement and compliance, and a considerable increase in the number of companies registered. The South African experience regarding corporate tax reform, which is examined in detail in chapter 7, should be of interest to Indian policy makers and more particularly to the government of Brazil, where requirements to generate public revenue have led to a vicious cycle of burgeoning tax rates, falling compliance, and increasing informality.

Using the World Bank's Doing Business Ranking Simulator to infer the potential impact of reforms on a country's ease of doing business, better rankings in the area "paying taxes" can be simulated for Brazil, India, and South Africa. The simulation suggests that, holding the data in all the other countries constant, India (currently ranked 134) could improve its ranking by seven positions if it were to reduce the number of average tax payments from the current 59 to the South African average of 30 payments. If Brazil were to reduce the total federal tax rate on profit from 71.7 percent to the South African rate of 38.3 percent, its ease of doing business ranking would move from 121st to 114th place.

In summary, tax is a common area of concern for business and hence a concern for policy makers in these emerging economies. Tax rate is a notable subject of complaint in all three. The tax system of Brazil is in urgent need of continued reform to reduce the administrative and financial burden imposed on firms. Althought tax policies in India and South Africa are less problematic, India needs

---

tax administration as a major constraint remained constant at 27 percent.

4. Only 19 percent of enterprises see tax rates as a serious problem, and only 11 percent see tax administration as a serious problem. This is lower than in all but three of the 52 investment climate surveys conducted in other countries by mid-2005. Until 1998, the corporate tax rate was 35 percent. It then declined to 30 percent, and the 2005 budget announced a reduction to 29 percent.

to lessen the number of tax payments made by firms, and South Africa needs to reduce the complexity of its system.

Foreign Trade and Exchange

International trade is recognized as an important engine of growth and development. Import of capital goods provides an important channel for technology transfer and knowledge adoption, particularly for developing countries that do not have large indigenous capabilities for research and development. The export of goods and services subjects firms to unparalleled competitive pressures and thereby ensures productive use of inputs. Government-imposed barriers to trade, which include not only tariffs and export promotion policies but also the efficiency of port, transportation, and customs infrastructure, can play a crucial role in determining a country's overall share of trade. While countries have generally lowered tariff barriers in conjunction with global and regional trade agreements, progress in improving trade infrastructure and reducing the uncertainty in international exchange has been slower, leaving lingering inefficiencies for trading firms.

Manufacturing exports from Brazil, India, and South Africa have all grown substantially in recent years, often exceeding the growth in world trade, although at slower rates than from China.[5] Nevertheless, exporting firms in all three countries are hampered by burdensome customs procedures, and this could be a common issue around which to discuss avenues for reform.[6] Onerous procedures significantly delay the time it takes for firms to receive ordered inputs or deliver exports, increasing the cost of input inventories in the former case and damaging business relationships in the latter. It is of concern that customs clearances are more time-consuming in Brazil and India than in most other business centers in their region (see table 3.2); for all three countries, they are about triple that of the Organisation for Economic Co-operation and Development (OECD) average. Among firms surveyed in the investment climate surveys, median reported times to clear customs are higher in all three countries than in either China or Indonesia (see figure 3.7). In Brazil, the reported level is particularly high, exceeding that of Kenya and Russia. Delays faced by exporting and

---

5   Between 1999 and 2004, manufacturing exports from Brazil grew at an average annual rate of 13 percent, compared to just 3 percent during the previous 15 years. The share of exports in Brazil's GDP has recently reached record levels, averaging 14.8 percent in 2000–04, compared to 9.7 percent in 1984–99.

6. Survey conducted by the Brazilian National Industrial Confederation found that the top four perceived barriers to the expansion of exports are the excessive bureaucracy at customs (41 percent of surveyed firms), the high costs of port services (37 percent), high costs of international transport (32 percent), and difficulty accessing export financing mechanisms (32 percent). In South Africa, about 22 percent of exporters rate customs and trade regulations as a serious obstacle.

Table 3.2
Procedural Requirements for Exporting and Importing a Standardized Cargo of Goods

City and region	Documents for export (number)	Signatures for export (number)	Time for export (days)	Documents for import (number)	Signatures for import (number)	Time for import (days)
São Paulo	7	8	39	14	16	43
Latin America	7.5	8.0	30.3	10.6	11.0	37.0
Mumbai	10	22	36	15	27	43
South Asia	8.1	12.1	33.7	12.8	24.0	46.5
Johannesburg	5	7	31	9	9	34
Sub-Saharan Africa	8.5	18.9	48.6	12.8	29.9	60.5

Source: World Bank (2006a).

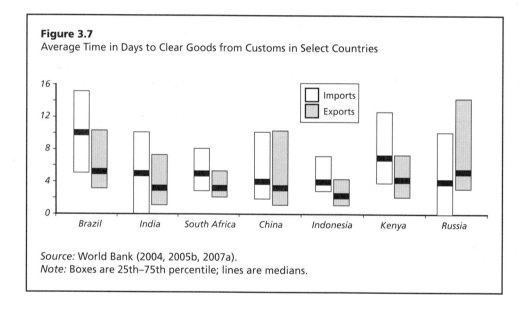

Figure 3.7
Average Time in Days to Clear Goods from Customs in Select Countries

Source: World Bank (2004, 2005b, 2007a).
Note: Boxes are 25th–75th percentile; lines are medians.

importing firms in Brazil and India also show substantial variation, making it difficult for firms to estimate the time it takes to ship goods to and from abroad, which leads to inevitable risks and expenses.

The costs and uncertainties imposed by the customs regimes of Brazil, India, and South Africa create significant bottlenecks to sustaining the recent expansion in international trade. Simple reforms can have an impact, however. Single windows can be established for traders, linking all government agencies involved in the clearance process, and risk-based management inspection systems can be computerized to allow customs staff to focus on cargo with a higher risk of faulty declaration. General government attitudes toward international trade can matter a lot, too. The large discrepancy in delays imposed on exports and imports in Brazil, for instance, represents embedded incentives to discourage substituting imports for locally produced manufactures. Recent reductions in average customs delays in India are thought to reflect growing appreciation among government bureaucracies for the economic value of international trade.[7]

The Benefits of Exporting: The Case of Brazil

The Brazil ICS confirms the long-run benefits of increasing exports: exporting firms experience higher employment and productivity growth, they invest more in fixed capital goods, and they pay higher wages. These findings show that, in comparison with nonexporters, exporters experience significant increases in their levels of employment, sales, productivity, capital per worker, and wages (see figure 3.8). Thus growth of exports can be expected to increase the average performance of the Brazilian manufacturing sector.

Moreover, econometric evidence supports the hypothesis that best-performing firms self-select into exporting. The differential characteristics of exporters could, in theory, emerge before or after initiating exporting activities. One interpretation of the results is that firms export if the expected increase in revenues derived from exporting surpasses the costs of entry. Thus larger and more productive firms would be more likely to export because they would either foresee higher expected increases in future revenues as a result of exporting or be

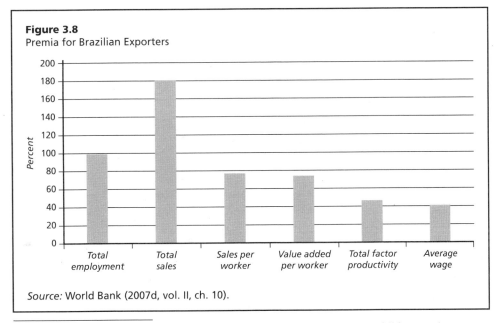

Figure 3.8
Premia for Brazilian Exporters

Source: World Bank (2007d, vol. II, ch. 10).

---

7. The average number of days needed for a shipment of inputs to clear customs fell from 10 days in 2000 to seven in 2003.

better able to overcome the entry barriers associated with initiating exports. Alternatively, one could explain these results by arguing that the differential characteristics of exporters are acquired through learning processes that take place after initiating sales in foreign markets—the so-called "learning-by-exporting" hypothesis.

A model of the determinants of entry into the exporting sector was constructed to test these hypotheses. Results favor the hypothesis that domestic success precedes exporting. Using a sample composed only of non-exporters, the analysis shows that larger firms and firms with higher productivity levels and shares of skilled employment are more likely to start exporting. It also finds that entry into foreign markets is more likely to occur among younger firms with lower capital stock per worker, is negatively related to the rates of capacity utilization, and has a positive relationship with exchange rate depreciation and the level of education of the firm managers. The high correlations that are found between exporting status and plant characteristics (for example, size, productivity, and share of skilled labor) are driven, at least in part, by the learning that takes place among future exporters while they are still oriented exclusively to the domestic market.

The findings that many of the superior traits of exporters precede their entry into foreign markets and that larger and more productive firms have a higher probability of exporting a higher share of their total output have important policy implications. They suggest that horizontal actions aimed at increasing the general level of productivity of the Brazilian manufacturing sector should be an important component of the policies to promote exporting growth. In addition, results indicate that export-promotion policies directed specifically to potential or existing exporters should focus on those firms or sectors that have already exhibited superior productivity.

Based on simulations using the Doing Business Ranking Simulator, India could improve its Doing Business ranking by 13 positions if it were to make trading across borders as easy as in Brazil.[8] Further, if Brazil were to reduce the average time necessary to comply with export procedures from 18 to 10 days, the OECD average, it could boost its ranking two places to 119, assuming that all other countries remain unchanged.

Since most firms are price takers in international markets, changes in exchange rates can dramatically affect revenues, particularly when currencies move contrary to expectations. Exporters and importers in Brazil and South Africa are particularly concerned about the volatility of the country's exchange rates (World Bank 2005b, 2007a). Since 2001, the Brazilian real and South African

---

8.   The ease of trading across borders looks at the procedural requirements for exporting and importing a standardized cargo of goods. Every official procedure is counted along with the time necessary for completion. According to data from the Doing Business Ranking Simulator, the ease of trading across borders is 0.37, 0.67, and 0.41 for Brazil, India, and South Africa, respectively.

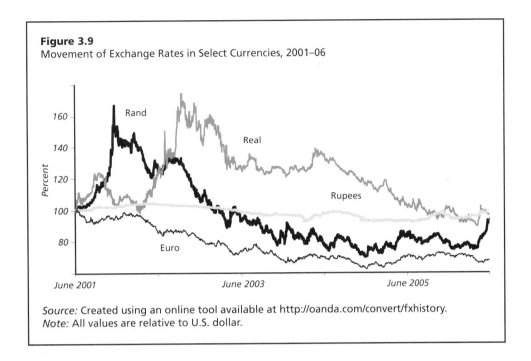

Figure 3.9
Movement of Exchange Rates in Select Currencies, 2001–06

Source: Created using an online tool available at http://oanda.com/convert/fxhistory.
Note: All values are relative to U.S. dollar.

rand have been among the most volatile of internationally traded currencies (see figure 3.9).[9] As noted in the investment climate assessment for South Africa, such instability has caused problems for South African firms trading abroad, which is reflected in the fact that 44 percent of exporters (and 76 percent of firms that export to the United States) cite macroeconomic instability as a serious constraint on their business, in spite of relatively low and stable rates of inflation and interest.[10] As in South Africa, macroeconomic instability is the second most widely cited concern of Brazilian firms, although, unlike in South Africa, such concern also spans high levels of interest rates (World Bank 2005b).

In summary, the analysis suggests that these emerging economies face some common macroeconomic problems where knowledge sharing on how best to pursue reform could be beneficial. The data point to the need for further reforms in Brazil, India, and South Africa to ease the burden of customs procedures and to make international trade more efficient for both importers and exporters. In addition, exchange rate volatility constrains the business operations of importers and exporters in Brazil and South Africa and thus needs to

9. A major depreciation between 2000 and 2002 caused the rand to fall 27 percent against the U.S. dollar, 26 percent against the British pound, and 28 percent against the euro. Over the next two years, the rand appreciated rapidly, rising 29 percent against the euro, 35 percent against the British pound, and 67 percent against the U.S. dollar.

10. Of firms that export goods to other OECD countries, 57 percent cite macroeconomic stability as a problem. Among exporters to South African Customs Union countries, which peg their currencies to the rand, only 17 percent of exporters rate macroeconomic instability as a concern.

be addressed by policy makers in both countries. However, this does not imply any preference for a fixed exchange rate regime versus a floating one, but rather the creation of enabling conditions for these markets to operate with reduced volatility. In the case of Brazil, the transition from a fixed to a floating exchange rate regime in 1999 proved to be effective in weathering the subsequent macroeconomic impacts in the domestic economy from serious disturbances in international markets.

4

Microeconomic Framework

The ability of firms to enter and exit the marketplace, expand and scale back capacity, and operate in an environment in which investors feel confident that their rights will be upheld and their outlays recouped is an essential precondition for ensuring the productive use of economic inputs and maximizing rates of economic growth. Although various forms of microeconomic regulation are essential to safeguard the public interest and to protect individuals from exploitation at the hands of unscrupulous operators, regulatory restrictions and bureaucratic requirements frequently transcend basic economic rationality and instead promote perverse outcomes that facilitate exploitation and undermine the public interest. Superfluous restrictions and inspections can impose severe administrative hassles for management, cause uncertainty in production processes, and result in direct costs in the form of irregular payments to officials. In this chapter, we examine and contrast the microeconomic frameworks and regulatory environments of Brazil, India, and South Africa and consider means by which policies and regulation could reduce microeconomic distortions, foster productivity, and promote capital investment. We begin by discussing the specifics of regulation in the three countries before turning to systems of enforcement.

Regulation

The procedures for entering and exiting a market determine the level of competition among producers and, therefore, microeconomic efficiency. Where market entry is restricted, incumbent firms are able to collect substantial rents through predatory pricing and face little incentive to innovate, undertake efficient investments, or employ their inputs in a productive manner. Similarly, excessive regulation can stifle the operation of factor markets and constrain firms from adjusting their scale to economically efficient levels. Finally, the framework for exiting a market, such as bankruptcy proceedings and protection of creditor rights, can either obstruct or support the resuscitation of ailing firms and make lenders wary of supporting entrepreneurs.

Entry of Firms

Countries differ significantly in the way they regulate the entry of new businesses (see table 4.1). In some, the process is straightforward, quick, and relatively inexpensive, allowing entrepreneurs to enter markets easily in response to opportunities. In other countries, firms must complete arduous and time-consuming processes populated by innumerable permit applications, notifications, inscriptions, verifications, and fees, encouraging entrepreneurs either to bribe officials in an effort to expedite the process or to enter the informal sector, with negative consequences for the tax base, fiscal balance, and economic growth. In most cities in India, registering a firm or a new property is a lengthy and costly proposition. Brazil performs a little better, particularly regarding the cost of registration, although there is room for improvement. Overall, South Africa performs better than most developing countries, although a little worse than the OECD average.

In most Brazilian cities, the time and cost of registering a new firm are not particularly onerous by Latin American standards. In all 13 cities surveyed, firm registration is less expensive than the regional average, and the duration of

Table 4.1

Bureaucratic and Legal Hurdles to Incorporate and Register a New Firm

City and region	Procedures (number)	Duration (days)	Cost (percent of gross national income per capita)	Minimum capital (percent of gross national income per capita)
São Paulo	17	152	10.1	0.0
Latin America	11	63	56.2	24.1
Mumbai	11	71	61.7	0.0
South Asia	8	35	40.5	0.8
Johannesburg	9	38	8.6	0.0
Sub-Saharan Africa	11	64	215.3	297.2
OECD	6.5	19.5	6.8	41.0

Source: World Bank (2006a).
Note: The data on starting a business are based on a survey of the required procedures for small- and medium-size companies dedicated to general commercial activities and services. The steps include obtaining necessary permits and licenses and completing official inscriptions, verifications, and notifications to enable the company to start operations.

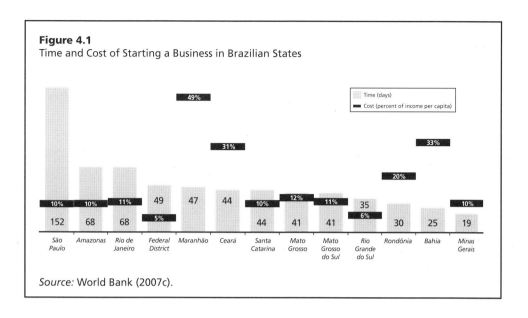

Figure 4.1
Time and Cost of Starting a Business in Brazilian States

Source: World Bank (2007c).

registration is shorter than the regional average in all but three of the cities.[1] However, substantial regional variation exists among states, reflecting the relatively onerous requirements imposed by some municipal authorities. In São Paulo the average amount of time spent is the longest in the country, at some six months, compared to just 19 days in Minas Gerais. Costs are lowest in the Federal District and Rio Grande do Sul, at between 5 and 6 percent of per capita income, and highest in the northeastern states of Maranhão, Bahia, and Ceará, at 49, 33, and 31 percent, respectively (see figure 4.1). Recent reforms have attempted to ease the procedural requirements for starting a business, and officials at the federal and subnational levels are taking measures to unify procedures, share information among agencies, and introduce online procedures. Particular success in this regard has been achieved in Minas Gerais, where the introduction of one-stop registration has located various agencies under a single roof and reduced the number of procedures to just 10.

Relative to the rest of Latin America, it is relatively difficult to register property in many Brazilian states. In the 12 states and the Federal District, an entrepreneur spends on average 61 days and 3.5 percent of the property value to register property (see figure 4.2). This ranks 17 out of 22 countries in Latin America. Even though the procedures for registering property are standardized on paper, costs and time vary considerably, even within regions. For instance, while it takes nearly three months and 2.4 percent of the value to register a property in Bahia, it takes under a month but 5.2 percent to register property

---

1. No minimum capital is required to start a business in Brazil, which reduces the cost for the entrepreneur. The largest determinants of cost are the printing of receipts for tax purposes, the municipal license, and registration fees.

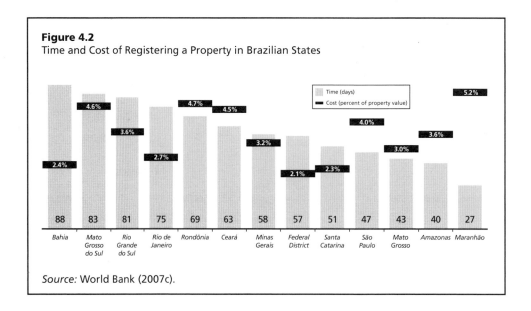

Figure 4.2
Time and Cost of Registering a Property in Brazilian States

Source: World Bank (2007c).

in Maranhão.[2] Overall, the Federal District and Santa Catarina are considered the easiest places to register property, while Mato Grosso do Sul, where the entrepreneur spends 83 days and 4.6 percent of the property value, is considered the most difficult.

Despite considerable reform of the regulations governing Indian industry since 1991, the time and cost required to register a business in the formal sector of Indian cities remain high by regional and international standards (see figure 4.3).[3] Entrepreneurs in Mumbai, for instance, must wait 71 days and pay some 62 percent of national per capita income in order to complete the registration process. By way of contrast, similar registration procedures in other South Asian business centers take only 35 days and 40 percent of per capita income. Unlike Brazil, the range of variation between Indian cities is not particularly large. Of the nine cities surveyed, procedures in Kolkata take the longest to complete (83 days), while Chandigarh and Bangalore provide for the quickest registration (57 days). Mumbai and Bangalore are the most expensive cities in which to start a business (62 percent of per capita income), while Bhubaneshwar is the cheapest (44 percent). During 2004–05, the Indian government undertook reforms to make starting a business easier for entrepreneurs, including automating the tax department's procedures and outsourcing to a private company the task of

---

2.   Time is measured from the start of the transaction to the sale-purchase agreement and finally the registration of the new title with the public registry.

3.   Early reforms include the removal of a policy of reserving certain industries for the public sector and the abolition of licensing requirements for private investment in many industries. The list of prohibited industries has recently been curtailed from 18 to three (atomic energy, railways, and military aircraft and warships), although India has yet to end its long-standing policy of reserving labor-intensive industries for small-scale producers.

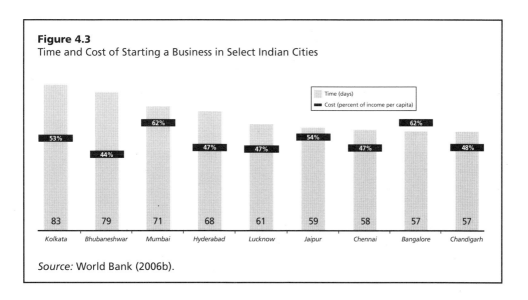

Figure 4.3
Time and Cost of Starting a Business in Select Indian Cities

Source: World Bank (2006b).

assigning firms a permanent account number (PAN) for tax payments. As a result, start-up time fell 18 days. Further reductions in delays are expected as implementation continues.

India's procedures for registering property, which average some six procedures and 67 days, are similar to those in countries throughout both South Asia and the developing world (see figure 4.4). Costs are relatively high in Indian cities, though, with registrations costing more, in terms of per capita income, than in all cities surveyed in Brazil. The duration of registrations in India exhibits substantial variation, but the range of costs is much more limited. The quickest city in which to register property is Bangalore (35 days), while Chandigarh is the slowest (132 days). Registrations cost the least in Mumbai (7.9 percent of property value) and the most in Hyderabad (14.9 percent). The high cost of registering property in India owes much to stamp duties, which tend to discourage formal transactions and promote rampant evasion, lowering government revenues as a result.[4] For instance, after halving stamp duties, the state of Maharastra experienced a 20 percent jump in revenues. Karnataka, meanwhile, has led the way in reducing the duration of registration through the computerization and rationalization of its property registry.

A related problem affecting Indian industry is the burden of licensing. To obtain permits and permissions to construct a warehouse costs nearly 700 percent of per capita income, rising up to more than 1,600 percent in Bangalore. It is also complex, requiring 20 procedures, and time-consuming, at 270 days,

4. Businesses use cumbersome and less secure ways to avoid taxes, such as replacing deeds with cooperative housing, long-term leases, agreements without possession, and transfers under court decrees.

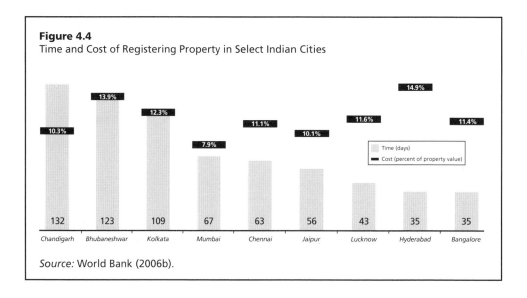

Figure 4.4
Time and Cost of Registering Property in Select Indian Cities

Source: World Bank (2006b).

substantially worse than the respective South Asian averages. The difference in the time taken and number of procedures required across states suggests that there are considerable gains to be realized from adopting best practices within India.[5] As an example, obtaining land use and construction permits for a property takes nearly 150 days and involves two departments in Mumbai but takes less than 40 days and involves one department in Hyderabad. Such improvements in certain regions help to explain why fewer Indian businesses reported licensing as a major obstacle in the 2006 ICS than in the 2003 survey.

The Doing Business database indicates that barriers to market entry in South Africa are low by standards of developing countries and just slightly above those of the OECD. However, this is in contrast to studies suggesting that the South African economy is highly concentrated and that there are high barriers to entry for both domestic and foreign firms. Consistent with this, firms in South Africa appear to be relatively profitable, despite having to pay high wages.

In summary, market entry issues are not as severe as other investment climate constraints in these three countries, as reflected in their lower ranking as obstacles in the national surveys. However, both Brazil and India face continued challenges. Entry regulations in Brazil are not particularly cumbersome by Latin American standards, but there is scope for substantial improvement if municipal authorities would follow the lead of states like Minas Gerais. Registering prop-

---

5.   The procedures that cause the greatest bottlenecks are obtaining land use permissions, building permits, power connections, water and sewerage connections, and final occupancy certificates. These are the responsibility of various municipal and state-level institutions. The difference in the time taken and number of procedures required across states suggests that there are considerable gains to be had from adopting best practices from other states.

erty is difficult in Brazil relative to the rest of Latin America, and this is an area that demands attention. Entrepreneurs wishing to enter markets in India are hamstrung by unusually high costs and lengthy procedures. It is also very expensive to acquire new property in Indian cities. Barriers to enter the market and acquire property in South Africa, meanwhile, are low in comparison to those in many developing countries.

Labor Regulation

For firms to be able to innovate and take advantage of new opportunities, it is important that entry and exit procedures be complemented by fluid factor markets that facilitate the transfer of inputs from low- to high-productivity applications. Owing to the social and political desirability of stabilizing employment levels, labor is one of the most heavily regulated factors of production, and all countries possess some legislation that purports to guarantee workers certain employment conditions. Labor regulation, however, can have unintended impacts on labor productivity, firm profitability, and broader macroeconomic outcomes. Instruments such as minimum wages, payroll taxes, and worker benefits usually raise the cost of employment, constrain hiring and firing, and may impede the movement of workers between positions. Labor legislation may also create incentives for workers to maintain or sever employment contracts, which, in turn, will affect the decisions of firms to invest in the labor force, with implications for the composition of a firm's labor force or a firm's budget for human capital investment and employee search. For all three countries, labor regulation is in need of reform. All have relatively rigid labor regulations that tend to discourage firms from hiring workers through formal channels, although Brazil's regulations provide particularly perverse incentives both for workers and for employers and promote a high degree of informality in the labor market (see table 4.2).

According to the analysis of the Doing Business team, labor regulations in Brazil are the 11th most restrictive in the world. Unusually burdensome legal regulations impede hiring in the formal sector and create problems for firms wishing to adjust their employees' hours of employment (see figure 4.5). In addition, firms must pay a quarter of a worker's average salary in hiring costs and pay the equivalent of three years of wages when they fire a worker, three times the regional average. It is not surprising, therefore, that labor regulation is among the top five constraints cited by Brazilian businesses and that some 88 percent of managers would change the size of their labor force if they faced no restrictions on worker dismissals, severance payments, and so forth.[6] The overwhelming

---

6.   The questionnaire asks business managers, "Given your current level of output, if you were free to choose without restrictions your current level of employment, what percent of the current

Table 4.2
Flexibility of Employment in Select Cities and Regions

City and region	Difficulty of hiring index	Rigidity of hours index	Difficulty of firing index	Rigidity of employment index	Hiring cost (percent of salary)	Firing costs (weeks of wages)
São Paulo	67	80	20	56	26.8	165.3
Latin America	41	51	30	40	15.9	62.9
Mumbai	56	40	90	62	12.3	79.0
South Asia	42	35	43	40	5.1	75.0
Johannesburg	56	40	60	52	2.6	37.5
Sub-Saharan Africa	48	63	48	53	11.8	53.4
OECD	30	50	28	36	20.7	35.1

Source: World Bank (2006a, 2007c, 2007d).

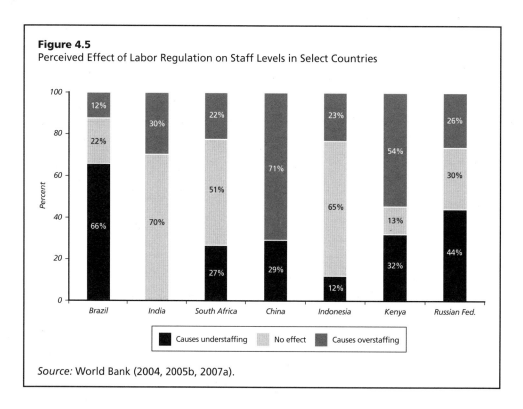

Figure 4.5
Perceived Effect of Labor Regulation on Staff Levels in Select Countries

Source: World Bank (2004, 2005b, 2007a).

proportion of those respondents report that a relaxation of labor rules would cause them to increase the number of workers they employ. Additional evidence indicates that employers are reticent to hire more skilled, and more expensive, workers, since the costs of labor legislation outweigh the benefits of higher labor productivity. A reduction in costly labor legislation could lead to both an

level would you choose?"

increase in employment and a change in the composition of the labor force toward a higher percentage of skilled workers. It also would improve Brazil's Doing Business ranking. Based on the Doing Business Ranking Simulator, Brazil would move its ranking from 121st to 119th if it would ease the "difficulty of hiring" workers to the regional average.[7]

Labor regulation was rated as an obstacle to the ease of doing business in both the 2003 and 2006 ICS in India, even though it did not rank among the leading five constraints. This reflects the fact that India's labor regulations are unusually complex.[8] Since independence in 1947, establishments with more than 100 workers have been required to secure state government permission before closing a plant or retrenching workers. This permission is rarely granted. The ability of firms to adjust employment is also restricted by collective agreements, making it difficult to shift workers not just between plants and locations but also between jobs in the same plant. To maintain flexibility in the allocation of manpower, firms commonly resort to a number of circumventions, such as the use of contract workers or, where this is precluded by state governments, the restriction of employment below the threshold level of 100 employees. The Doing Business report confirms that all facets of India's labor regulations are more stringent than the average for South Asian countries (World Bank 2007d). The "difficulty of firing" workers in India, for instance, is rated 90 out of 100, more than double the regional average. Firms must pay 79 weeks of salary in notice, severance, and penalties to dismiss a worker, compared with a regional average of 75 weeks and East Asian and OECD averages of 44 and 35 weeks, respectively. Among Indian firms, 30 percent report that they would lay off more workers if regulations were less onerous, with the average firm reporting that they employ 11 percent more workers than they desire. Although this number is high relative to Brazil, it was higher in the 2000 ICS: 17 percent. The change is thought to be due to increasing government reluctance to enforce the more intrusive provisions of existing laws. However, labor regulation remains a real concern: it was among the top six constraints most frequently cited by business in all of the states of India in the 2006 ICS. Firms resent restrictions on hiring and firing practices, including restrictions on hiring casual or temporary labor. There is clear room for improvement. According to the Doing Business Ranking Simulator, India could advance six positions in the ranking from 134th to 128th if it could reduce the "difficulty of firing workers" to the regional average.[9]

---

7. According to World Bank (2006a), the regional average for "ease of employing workers" is rated 34.4 (percentile). Brazil is rated 66.7 (percentile).

8. World Bank (2006b) reports that 47 central laws and 157 state regulations directly affect labor markets, many of which are inconsistent and overlapping. As a result, it is almost impossible either for firms or workers to be aware of their rights and obligations or for enforcement authorities to ensure compliance.

9. In 2006 India was rated 70th on the "difficulty of firing" index. The South Asian average was 37.5.

Generally, labor regulations are less constraining in South Africa than in Brazil and India, but more rigid than in the OECD. Firms in South Africa cite labor regulation as the third most important factor constraining economic expansion, behind worker skills and macroeconomic stability (World Bank 2007a). The Doing Business data confirm that hiring and firing workers in South Africa are more legally complicated than the regional average and significantly more so than in the OECD. However, the costs of hiring in South Africa are relatively low, at just 2.6 percent of the annual salary. The costs of firing are also in line with those in OECD countries.

In summary, labor regulation is problematic in all three countries. Regulations in Brazil and India are very complex and impose substantial constraints on the ability of firms to adjust their work force in response to market conditions. In South Africa, regulation appears to be less stringent than in Brazil or India, but still more so than the OECD average, and is seen as a major constraint by local firms. That said, South Africa's experience with minimizing the costs of hiring and firing workers is potentially highly instructive to Brazil, India, and other emerging economies.

Exit of Firms

Procedures for the exit of firms are important both to resuscitate ailing companies, where appropriate, and to provide creditors with speedy and inexpensive recovery of their assets once firms have irrevocably failed. Where bankruptcy procedures do not fulfill these goals, the function of markets can be disrupted. If creditors' rights are not upheld, for instance, financial institutions are more reluctant to loan to firms, resulting in high interest rates and low productivity across the economy.

Of the three countries, none has exemplary bankruptcy proceedings. Although not among the constraints most often cited by companies, bankruptcy is another issue where all have room to improve and should seek to learn from the reform efforts of others.

The average time to complete procedures and recover assets in South Africa is short, at just two years, although the speed is achieved only at significant cost, some 18 percent of the estate, which is more than double the cost of a similar proceeding in the OECD. The rate of recovery of assets by shareholders afforded by the South African legal system, at 34 percent, is high for developing countries, but around a third of that achieved in industrial economies.

In both Brazil and India, the recovery of assets takes, on average, a staggering 10 years, well over double the norm in both of their regions and longer than anywhere else in the world (see table 4.3). While procedures are reasonably inexpensive in both countries, the rate of recovery achieved by

Table 4.3

Efficiency of Bankruptcy Proceedings

City and region	Average time to complete procedure (years)	Cost of bankruptcy proceedings (percent of estate)	Percent of assets recovered from insolvent firms
São Paulo	10.0	9.0	0.5
Latin America	3.5	17.0	28.2
Mumbai	10.0	9.0	12.8
South Asia	4.2	7.3	19.7
Johannesburg	2.0	18.0	34.0
Sub-Saharan Africa	3.3	19.5	16.1
OECD	1.5	7.4	73.8

Source: World Bank (2006a).

both systems is low. In India, the figure is 13 percent, well below the regional average of 20 percent. In Brazil, creditors can expect to recover just half a percent of the value of their assets, compared to 28 percent across Latin America generally.

Part of the problem in Brazil is that the law has long prohibited creditors from seizing and selling collateral on default without the consent of the debtor, unless a lawsuit is filed and the court rules in favor of the plaintiff. Even with this ruling, debtors have various options for appeal, during which time they retain control over the assets. In India, defaulting borrowers take refuge under the Sick Industrial Companies Act in order to avoid payment to creditors. Insolvency procedures are protracted further by the lack of adequate specialized resources among courts and tribunals and by the requirement that firms employing more than 100 workers must seek the permission of the state government before closing a site or retrenching workers, something that state authorities rarely grant. As a result, bankruptcy procedures in India vary significantly from state to state (see figure 4.6). The least effective system is that of West Bengal, which takes 20 years on average, with an average recovery of just 5 percent. Karnataka's system, in contrast, takes eight years and recovers 17 percent of creditor's assets. Both Brazil and India have undertaken recent reforms of their bankruptcy system that are of potential interest for policy makers in other countries. Brazil's changes, introduced in 2005, created a reorganization procedure that both helps viable enterprises to stay afloat and gives secured creditors more influence over the process and gives priority to their collateral. The reform faced its first test in June 2005, when the Brazilian carrier Varig filed for bankruptcy. In little more than a year, Varig's assets were sold to a new owner, and bankruptcy is nearly complete.

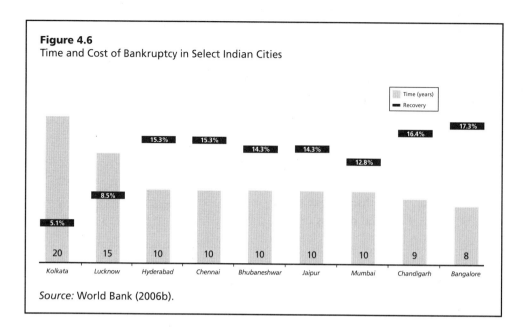

Figure 4.6
Time and Cost of Bankruptcy in Select Indian Cities

Source: World Bank (2006b).

Enforcement

Enforcing business laws and regulations is a fine art. Businesses require supportive, but not intrusive, forms of public administration. Officials inspecting compliance with taxation and regulatory policies must apply the law consistently and in a manner that does not encourage the exaction of bribes or rents from enterprises, either for real or for imagined violations. Similarly, the courts must enforce commercial contracts in an expeditious manner that reassures investors that their property rights will be upheld.

Enforcement of Contracts

Almost all forms of legitimate economic activity and exchange are reliant, albeit implicitly, on the enforcement of contracts. Yet in many developing countries, judicial remedies for those seeking enforcement of contracts are slow, costly, and often unreliable (see table 4.4). An essential step in promoting economic development is thus to enhance the confidence of economic actors in the capability of the judiciary to enforce contracts. The results captured in the investment climate assessments and the Doing Business data help us to assess the efficiency of contract enforcement by providing information on the complexity of procedures, the time and cost to enforce a contract, and the confidence of firms in the local judiciary.[10]

---

10. The cost of judicial access is composed of court expenses and attorney fees, whereas duration measures the time necessary to file a case, obtain a ruling from the judge, and execute a decision.

Of the three countries, managers in South Africa seem most confident that firms will uphold property rights, followed by managers in India and then in Brazil (see figure 4.7). The high confidence shown by firms in South Africa is validated by the Doing Business data, which demonstrate that contract enforcement is relatively efficient in South Africa's main business center of Johannesburg. It takes only nine months, which is close to the OECD average, and costs only 11.5 percent of the total value of debt, a level similar that of courts in developed countries.

In contrast, in Brazil the duration of contract enforcement is particularly lengthy, around 18 months, compared to less than eight months in OECD countries (see figure 4.8). The process is often prolonged by multiple appeals, the inexperience of courts in dealing with commercial cases, and strategies of brink-

Table 4.4
Burden to Resolve Payment Disputes through the Legal System

City and region	Procedures (number)	Duration (days)	Cost (percent of debt)
São Paulo	24	546	15.5
Latin America	35	461	23.3
Mumbai	40	425	43.1
South Asia	30	386	17.7
Johannesburg	26	277	11.5
Sub-Saharan Africa	36	439	41.6
OECD	20	226	10.6

Source: World Bank (2006a).

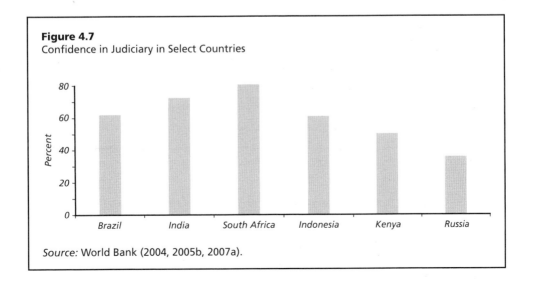

Figure 4.7
Confidence in Judiciary in Select Countries

Source: World Bank (2004, 2005b, 2007a).

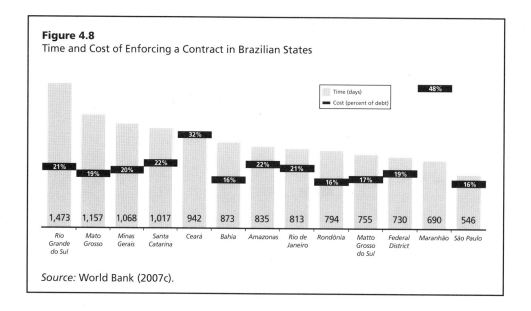

Figure 4.8
Time and Cost of Enforcing a Contract in Brazilian States

Source: World Bank (2007c).

manship among claimants.[11] As a result of this process, small businesses are particularly keen to avoid judicial processes as much as possible and, in surveys, are not prone to trust the courts to protect their property rights and adjudicate their contract disputes.[12] Substantial variation exists within Brazil, however, as to the efficiency of judicial enforcement. Access to justice is cheapest in São Paulo, where it costs 15.5 percent of the value of debt to enforce a contract, compared with 48.3 percent in Maranhão. Although contract enforcement is lengthy in São Paulo by international standards, the business center outperforms other major cities in Brazil by a substantial margin. In Rio Grande do Sul, it takes more than four years to enforce a contract.

Indian managers, in general, express a relatively high level of confidence in the judiciary. However, as with Brazil, the actual process is often lengthy and costly by international standards (see figure 4.9). In India's major business center of Mumbai, it takes more than 14 months to enforce a contract, nearly double that in China. The total cost of enforcement is a whopping 43 percent of the value of debt, which significantly undermines the rationality of pursuing judicial recourses. Other major Indian cities fare better in the cost of enforcement, but much worse in duration. In Lucknow (Uttar Pradesh), it takes more than three years to enforce a contract, while in Chandigarh and Kolkata it takes more than 2.5 years. The cost of contract enforcement, however, is relatively

11. World Bank (2007c) reports that in Brazil 88 percent of commercial cases are appealed, compared to 13 percent in Argentina, 17 percent in Peru, and 30 percent in Mexico.

12. According to World Bank (2005b), "Between 25 percent and 28 percent of micro firms do not believe that courts will protect their property rights. For large firms, this distrust in courts is only 5 percent."

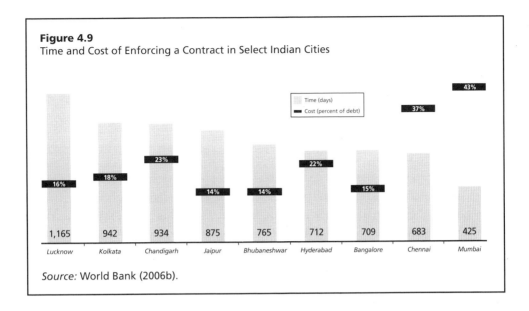

Figure 4.9
Time and Cost of Enforcing a Contract in Select Indian Cities

Source: World Bank (2006b).

cheap in Bangalore, Bhubaneshwar, and Jaipur, at around 15 percent of the total value of debt. The generally long delays and high costs in getting contracts enforced encourage firms to resolve disputes informally, a fact confirmed by the results of the investment climate survey. In order to resolve this situation, World Bank (2006b: 28) recommends that "rules of civil procedure can be amended to restrict the adjournments judges can give and to allow judges to impose strict time limits and a trial calendar on the parties." In order to expedite the enforcement of judgments, which take up the vast majority of time spent moving a case through the courts, the report authors recommend "scrapping the public monopoly on executing judges' rulings" and allowing "licensed private enforcement agents" to move into the business.

Both India and Brazil could improve their Doing Business rankings, if they would reform their system of contract enforcement, according to the Doing Business Ranking Simulator. If India would improve its "ease of enforcing contracts" from the current level of 0.92 (percentile) to the Brazilian level of 0.60 (percentile), it would rank 119th, an improvement of 15 places. Brazil could benefit from improving its ease of enforcing contracts to the East Asian and Pacific average. Under this scenario, Brazil would improve its Doing Business ranking by four positions.[13]

In summary, while enforcing commercial contracts is not a significant problem within the three countries, both Brazilian and Indian firms report that enforcement is generally lengthy and expensive, although substantial variation exists within both countries. This suggests that both countries could benefit

13. In 2006 Brazil was ranked 121st.

from reviewing more successful domestic procedures of their own states as well as policies in other emerging economies, such as South Africa, where contract enforcement is relatively efficient.

Enforcement of Regulation

All systems of government regulation require systems of enforcement. However, the officials, bureaucracies, and judicial entities responsible for such enforcement do not always do so in ways that are efficient, transparent, predictable, or even honest. Particularly where regulation is complex or not particularly accessible, the functionaries involved have room for discretion, leaving business operators in an uncertain and often precarious position. This inevitably raises the costs of doing business, both indirectly in terms of preparing for multiple eventualities of interpretation and enforcement and directly in terms of irregular payments to unscrupulous officials seeking private gain.

Both Brazil and India possess relatively complex systems of regulation that tend to encourage rent seeking by government officials and impose administrative costs on firms in ensuring compliance. Two-thirds of Brazilian firms, for instance, report that corruption is a major or severe impediment to business operation, while Indian firms cite corruption among their primary concerns, although the percentage dropped from 38 percent in 2003 to 28 percent in 2006. The incidence of firms reporting bribes also fell in this period, but remains high in absolute terms. Informal payments appear to be the norm for availing basic services, permits, and licenses.[14] Furthermore, the proportion of firms in Brazil that report officials' interpretation of laws to be consistent and reliable is relatively low and well below the proportion reported in India and South Africa (see figure 4.10). The investment climate surveys also ask firms about the frequency of annual inspection visits and the amount of management time spent complying with regulation and dealing with government officials. Overall, Brazil and India do relatively well on the frequency of inspections, with national averages for both countries at around seven or eight visits a year, which is much less than the average 28 visits reported in China. Brazilian managers also spend a relatively minimal amount of time dealing with regulation, less than in China or Kenya (see figure 4.11). In India, though, the figure is much higher than in Brazil, Indonesia, Russia, or South Africa and varies widely by region. Regulation and its associated enforcement seem to be less of a problem in South Africa than in the other two countries, although some South African managers report spending up to 15 percent of their time dealing with regulatory issues.

---

14. Government officials requested or expected gifts in 56 percent of all inspections, according to responses in the 2006 ICS for India.

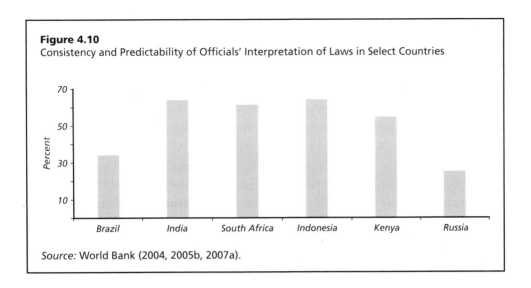

Figure 4.10
Consistency and Predictability of Officials' Interpretation of Laws in Select Countries

Source: World Bank (2004, 2005b, 2007a).

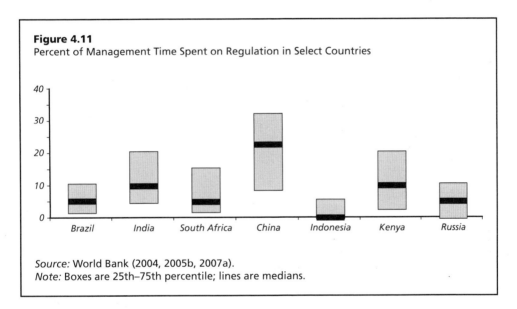

Figure 4.11
Percent of Management Time Spent on Regulation in Select Countries

Source: World Bank (2004, 2005b, 2007a).
Note: Boxes are 25th–75th percentile; lines are medians.

Firms in the north and southeast of Brazil are exposed to the highest overall inspection burden—some 30 hours on average by federal, state, and municipal authorities, compared to an average of 14 hours in the center-west region. Overall, managers in the northeastern states of Bahia, Ceará, and Paraíba spend the least amount of time dealing with regulations, followed by managers in the center-west, south, and southeast. Those in the northern state of Amazonas spend the most amount of time, which may be explained by the widespread use of fiscal incentives in that state. The frequency of inspections also varies significantly with firm size. Large firms receive, on average, four times as many annual inspections as micro firms. For micro firms, inspections by municipal environmental authorities are most burdensome, while, for medium- and large-size firms, the federal health ministry and labor and social security agencies make the most frequent inspections.[15]

Indian business regulation is laid out mainly by federal law, although state governments, and the individual inspectors they appoint, are given considerable discretion in enforcement (see figure 4.12). As a result, the "license raj" at the center does not necessarily have a significant impact on the "inspection raj," who presides at the state level. There is accordingly significant variation between Indian states in the burden of compliance with regulation. In Gujarat, which is generally considered to be one of the more investment-friendly Indian states, managers spend nearly a quarter of their time dealing with regulation, compared to managers in the poorer states of Madhya Pradesh and Uttar Pradesh, who spend just 7–8 percent. Firms in Madhya Pradesh also report the lowest number of inspections (just two per year), while firms in West Bengal and Kerala report the most (13 and 14 per year, respectively).

In summary, the complex nature of regulation in Brazil and India has led to frequent instances of official corruption. In India, corruption is a leading concern, while two-thirds of Brazilian firms think it is a problem. Firms in Brazil and India do, however, spend less time dealing with regulation than their peers in China, although substantial regional variation exists in both countries. Regu-

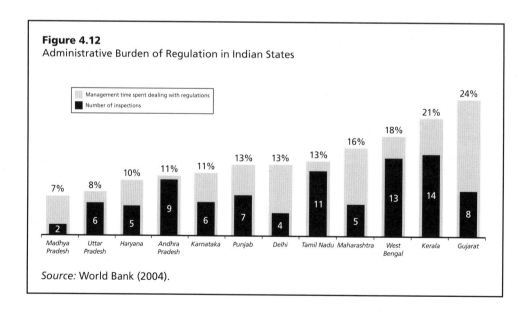

Figure 4.12
Administrative Burden of Regulation in Indian States

Source: World Bank (2004).

---

15. Federal and municipal health departments are the most frequent inspectors, making an annual average of 1.7 inspections per business. Labor and Social Security follow, with an average of 1.3 inspections per business a year. The Federal Environmental Agency, Fire and Building Safety, and Standards are the least frequent inspectors.

lation and its associated enforcement seem to be less of a problem in South Africa than in the other two countries, although some South African managers report spending up to 15 percent of their time dealing with regulatory issues.

5

Enabling Environment for Growth

A country's enabling infrastructure consists of the normal set of services, factors, and conditions that firms require to establish operations and engage in production and exchange. As such, it encompasses areas as diverse as the availability of credit, the quality of a country's transportation network, and public safety. Often, the quality of a country's enabling infrastructure is affected by historical and institutional factors exogenous to the orientation of government policy, at least over the short term. South Africa, for instance, suffers from high crime rates arising from the legacy of apartheid-era policies and the associated socioeconomic inequalities; transportation infrastructure in India is still very much reliant on an extensive rail network constructed while the country was still under colonization; and the availability and cost of credit in Brazil are affected by the legacy of macroeconomic imbalances. In this chapter, we examine and contrast the quality of the enabling environment in Brazil, India, and South Africa, including assessments of key constraints for one or all of the economies, such as access to finance, physical infrastructure, and the cost and availability of skilled labor, as well as the issue of crime.

Investment Climate and Firm Location

A good investment climate is essential for a country or a region to attract investments and new firms. A country's unique attributes or "geography" (for example, climate, endowment of natural resources, distance from important markets, and size) are also important, as are the so-called agglomeration economies. The agglomeration of firms from the same industry (for example, localization economies) creates externalities that increase productivity for all firms in that industry. These benefits include sharing sector-specific inputs, skilled labor, knowledge, intra-industry linkages, and opportunities for efficient subcontracting. In addition to own-industry localization economies, inter-industry externalities (economic diversities) also influence firms' location decisions and productivity.

The 2004 investment climate assessment for India explored a location model applied to 40 Indian cities in an effort to assess the relative importance of these variables. Building on previous work in regional economics and industrial organization, the report measures the role of both classical determinants of firm location (for example, input costs, access to markets, and transportation infrastructure) and network effects (for example, inter-industry spillovers and intra-industry agglomeration effects). Properly identifying each of these effects and determining how each one differs by industry will have important implications for predicting the consequences of both explicit policies and regional endowments to attract economic activities across Indian cities.

The main findings show positive and statistically significant estimates for own-industry concentration variables, confirming the importance of agglomeration economies for firm location in India. They also confirm the importance of investment climate variables. Regulation and corruption are also determinants of business locations across Indian cities. Cities where firms in general face lower regulatory burdens are likely to receive more investment and have higher shares of manufacturing activity. Regarding factor prices, results clearly show that the price of electricity is the most important factor determining the attractiveness of individual cities in India. The availability and reliability of infrastructure are major determinants of business profitability. Thus intercity differentials in infrastructure are found to have important consequences for where firms will locate across the national urban system.

Regarding infrastructure, an interesting result was obtained in a follow-up survey conducted in 2006 with 440 Brazilian firms that responded to the 2003 ICS. The survey asked firms specific questions on their location decisions (World Bank 2007e). According to survey responses, infrastructure is the factor that has the greatest effect on firms' location decisions. This is a bit surprising, since, according to the ICS for Brazil, infrastructure is not ranked as a top constraint on growth (see figure 5.1). This can probably be explained by the fact that location is considered a given by firms when consulted about constraints on growth. That the respondents in the 2006 ICS for India list electricity supply as the largest constraint they face serves to emphasize the scale of the problem across the country. The truth is that, other things equal, a region endowed with infrastructure is advantageously positioned vis-à-vis other regions to attract new firms.

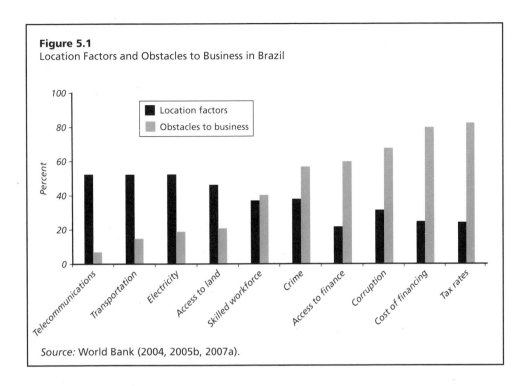

Figure 5.1
Location Factors and Obstacles to Business in Brazil

Source: World Bank (2004, 2005b, 2007a).

Access to Finance

Finance is a fundamental component of any business operation. Without inexpensive and readily accessible means by which to acquire it, firms are often precluded from expanding, engaging in research and development, and even surviving during unfavorable economic times. While the availability and cost of credit are often influenced by historical and institutional factors, government policies have a pronounced impact. Financial taxation, inefficient bankruptcy procedures, and directed credit policies all tend to raise interest rates well above what they otherwise would be, making it difficult for firms to grow and, in some cases, even survive.

Accessing finance is a major problem for firms in Brazil; three-quarters of managers cite the cost of finance as a constraint on the growth of their business. Over half of Brazilian firms that claim to need loans opt not to apply, citing reasons such as complicated application procedures, high interest rates, and strict collateral requirements. In China and India, the corresponding figures are just 32 and 16 percent of firms, respectively. As noted in the investment climate assessment for Brazil (World Bank 2005b), although lending rates in Brazil have fallen over the past decade, they remain above 50 percent, which is extremely

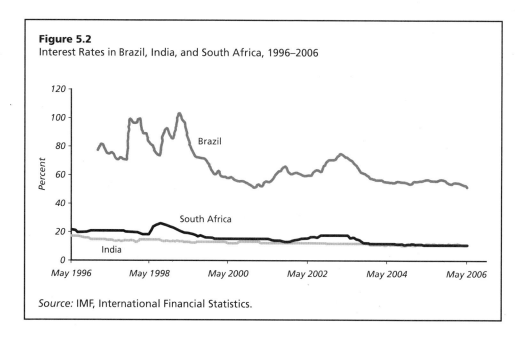

Figure 5.2
Interest Rates in Brazil, India, and South Africa, 1996–2006

Source: IMF, International Financial Statistics.

high by international standards (see figure 5.2).[1] Interest rate spreads are also significantly greater in Brazil than in similar middle-income economies. The wide rate spreads and high lending rates are commonly attributed to unfavorable macroeconomic conditions, particularly the high level of public sector debt, although weak creditor rights, the lack of banking competition, and high levels of financial taxation are also a significant part of the explanation.[2]

In obtaining finance from banks and other formal financial institutions, firm size clearly matters in Brazil. While three-quarters of large firms that declare a need for credit have bank loans, just 44 percent of small firms and 36 percent of micro firms have them. The reason for this is that financial institutions tend to view lending to smaller firms as a risky proposition owing to the common use of informal procedures and the lack of reliable information on their financial situation.[3] This uncertainty is reflected in the wide dispersion of interest rates

---

1. The median nominal interest rate reported by enterprises surveyed in the Brazil investment climate survey was 40 percent, higher than in Senegal (12 percent), Poland (12 percent), Kenya (15 percent), and South Africa (11 percent).

2. Brazil's central bank breaks down spread into cost of default (17 percent), taxes (29 percent), profits (41 percent), and administrative expenses (13 percent). High default costs reflect the effects of weak credit rights, poor screening of borrowers, and insufficient protection of creditors due to imperfections in both the legal system and juridical practice. The large share of profits and administrative expenses reflects the lack of competitiveness in the credit market and the cost of direct credit to the economy. The high taxation on the financial sector (and on the economy in general) is in large part due to the inability to reduce public expenditure.

3. According to indicators garnered through the investment climate assessments, such as informality, unreported sales, and the use of external auditing, Brazilian SMEs are less transparent

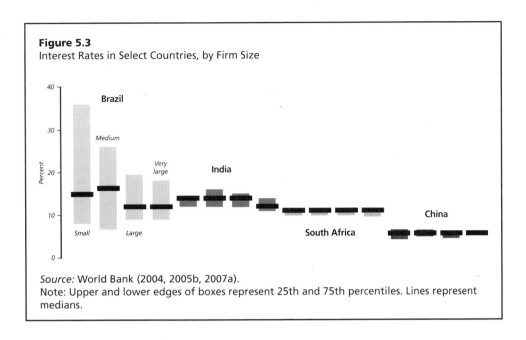

Figure 5.3
Interest Rates in Select Countries, by Firm Size

Source: World Bank (2004, 2005b, 2007a).
Note: Upper and lower edges of boxes represent 25th and 75th percentiles. Lines represent medians.

charged to Brazilian small and medium enterprises (see figure 5.3). Firms that have a bank loan do not appear to be more productive than those that have applied for a loan and been rejected, however, underscoring the information asymmetries in the credit market.

In order to lower interest rates in Brazil, it is essential to devise sound macroeconomic policies and reduce public debt. Creditor rights have been strengthened through the enactment of new laws on bankruptcy, and it is critical for enforcement in order to establish trust in these new protections. Further measures that would reduce the magnitude of spreads include easing the burden of financial taxation, including indirect taxation such as reserve requirements and directed credit. In order for smaller firms to gain access to credit, a crucial step is to undertake regulatory reform to ease the costs of operating in the formal sector.

Access to external financing is a major issue for firms in India, particularly for small firms (World Bank 2004).[4] The problem is somewhat different in India than in Brazil, though, as it relates as much to access as to cost, reported as a major obstacle to business in both the 2003 and 2006 ICS. While as many as 75 percent of small businesses in Brazil have bank credit lines or overdraft

than their larger counterparts. As a result, Brazilian micro firms have the greatest rate of rejected loan applications.

4.   Some 27 percent of respondents rate access to finance as a major to severe obstacle to business operations or growth.

facilities, only 57 percent of firms had an overdraft facility in India in 2003.[5] Prior to 1997, Indian small and medium enterprises (SMEs) were quite reliant on debt financing both from banks and from other financial institutions, but changes in policies and regulations have caused the nonbank financial sector to shrink and for bank credit to SMEs to fall sharply. Presently, the limited debt financing available to Indian SMEs is of short maturity and relatively costly compared with the debt financing available to SMEs in other countries. Firm complaints focus on the inability to borrow at the going rate due to nonprice barriers and complex and unpredictable loan processing. Based on the Doing Business Ranking Simulator, India could improve its "ease of doing business" rank by nine places (from 134th to 125th), if it would improve its ranking for ease of getting credit from the country's current level to that of South Africa.

As in Brazil, much of the financing constraints faced by SMEs in India arises from credit market and institutional imperfections that raise transaction costs and default risks. Specifically, financial institutions in India lack adequate means of reliably assessing the creditworthiness of SMEs, performing risk management, or undertaking monitoring, and they face legal difficulties in using land as collateral.[6] As discussed in chapter 4, delays and uncertainties associated with the bankruptcy framework in India make it difficult for troubled firms to exit the market and weaken the ability of creditors in to enforce collateral and recover loans. However, the situation seems to be improving. Several commercial banks and credit information service providers have established the Credit Information Bureau of India Limited (CIBIL), which should help to deepen the amount and quality of credit information available. The implementation of the Securitization and Reconstruction of Financial Assets and Enforcement of Security Interest Act (SARFAESI) has significantly reduced the time needed to enforce collateral. To reinforce this progress, further action is needed to assure creditors that their collateral will be given priority inside and outside of bankruptcy and that they will be able to enforce collateral agreements without recourse to the judicial system.

Compared to firms in Brazil, India, and many other developing countries, firms in South Africa do not view either access to or cost of finance as serious obstacles to the operations and growth of enterprises.[7] Objective data generally support the perception-based data, particularly with respect to the cost of financing. Real interest rates are relatively low, at around 5 percent, compared

---

5.   This figure fell to 53 percent in 2006, although this fall is attributable largely to the inclusion of firms from lower-income Indian states in the 2006 ICS. For panel firms, the proportion remained constant at 60 percent.

6.   According to the Doing Business database, for instance, the scope, access, and quality of credit information available to lenders in India lag behind those in Nepal, Pakistan, and Sri Lanka.

7.   In 17 of 49 low- and middle-income countries, more than 40 percent of enterprises report that finance is a major or very severe problem. In South Africa fewer than 20 percent of enterprises rate access to finance as either a major or a very severe obstacle.

with many developing countries.[8] As noted in the investment climate assessment, firms in South Africa finance less investment through banks than firms in China, Kenya, Senegal, or Poland, and fewer firms have access to overdraft facilities than in either Brazil or Kenya. However, this may reflect the preferences of South African firms. Most firms that do not have loans report that they do not want or need a loan, and very few firms have been rejected for a loan. One potential explanation is that South African firms rely more heavily on retained earnings to finance both investment and working capital (World Bank 2007a).[9]

In summary, access to and the cost of credit are major issues for firms in Brazil and India, particularly those that are small. Interest rates in Brazil are extremely high, particularly for SMEs, and access to finance is often restricted due to the widespread use of informal procedures among small firms. SMEs in India also lack access to credit due to nonprice barriers, including high collateral requirements and the absence of reliable credit information, although recent innovations should help to improve this. Access to credit does not seem to be a major concern for firms in South Africa, suggesting that closer review of its credit policies could offer insights for policy makers in Brazil, India, and other emerging economies.

Physical Infrastructure

Infrastructure services are a key component of production, affecting the cost and ability of firms to complete production, to receive inputs and deliver goods, and to communicate with suppliers and customers. While some firms can assume the cost of providing some of these services privately, most are under the purview of the government and can be readily addressed by reform measures.

In Brazil, while it seems clear that the poor quality of transport and electricity provision is negatively affecting firm performance, infrastructure is not among the most often cited obstacles to growth.[10] This is probably related to the fact that despite a major collapse in infrastructure investment, Brazil's infrastructure sector still performs at reasonable levels compared to that of the rest of Latin America.[11] Unreliable supplies of electricity impose a heavy burden on

---

8. The median nominal interest rate reported by enterprises surveyed in the investment climate survey for South Africa is 11 percent, lower than in Senegal (12 percent), Poland (12 percent), Kenya (15 percent), and Brazil (40 percent).

9. When asked why they have not applied for a loan, most of these firms report either that they do not need a loan (72 percent), that they receive financing from their parent company (10 percent), or that they do not want to incur debt (10 percent). The role of non-banking financial companies in South Africa may also be another factor in the lower demand for loans.

10. Brazilian firms lose approximately 3.5 percent of their annual sales as a result of poor infrastructure services. Firms that experience losses lose around 17 percent of their annual sales.

11. Average investment in electricity generation is less than a third of its level during the 1970s, while investments in transportation are about a quarter of their level in the 1970s.

Table 5.1
Effectiveness of Public Power Supply in Select Countries

Country	Days to connect to public grid	Percent of output lost to outages	Percent of generator ownership	Percent of power from generator
Brazil	10	2.5	17.0	1.6
Peru	7	3.2	28.2	5.9
India	45	10.0	63.5	19.1
China	6	2.0	20.1	1.6
South Africa	4	0.9	9.4	0.2
Kenya	21	9.1	69.7	14.0

Source: World Bank (2004, 2005b, 2007a).
Note: Data are for manufacturing firms only. "Days" represent median values.

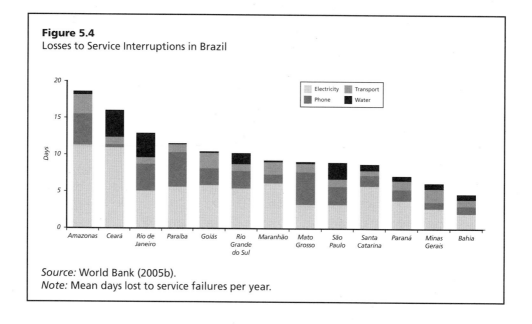

Figure 5.4
Losses to Service Interruptions in Brazil

Source: World Bank (2005b).
Note: Mean days lost to service failures per year.

firms in Brazil, creating greater production delays than failures in other public utilities (see table 5.1). The reliability of the power supply varies significantly within Brazil, however, and this is reflected in strong regional disparities in the effects of service failures on firms (see figure 5.4). Firms in the north (particularly Amazonas) and northeast (particularly Ceará) report significant losses of production arising from power outages.[12] To mitigate the problem of uncertain supply, around 17 percent of Brazilian firms own power generators (see figure 5.5). In Mato Grosso and Amazonas, more than 35 percent of firms own generators. Although utilities in the north and northeast are relatively unreliable, firms

---

12. The regional pattern of outages observed for water, telephone, and transport services is similar to that of electricity, although with a smaller magnitude.

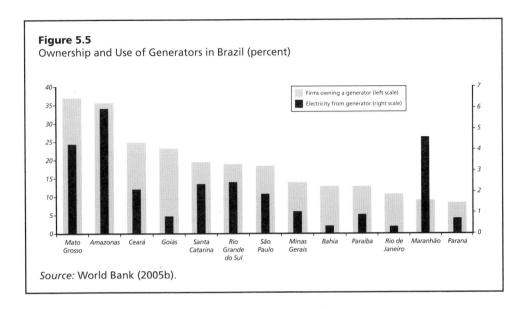

Figure 5.5
Ownership and Use of Generators in Brazil (percent)

Source: World Bank (2005b).

in the south and southeast must wait the longest to get connected to mainline services. For instance, while the median time for a new firm in Rio de Janeiro to receive power is some 25 days, establishing a connection takes only five days in Maranhão (World Bank 2005b).

The cost of transporting goods to market is significant in Brazil, representing one-third of firms' average operational costs. To a significant extent, this reflects the poor and deteriorating condition of the 58,000 kilometers of paved roads, which carry some 70 percent of transported goods. More than a quarter of the network is in poor condition, and this is estimated to add half a billion U.S. dollars annually to the costs of operating vehicles.[13] Costs vary systematically across Brazilian regions, with firms in the center-west region suffering losses of consignment cargo in transit twice as high as firms in the north.[14] Among all regions in Brazil, the highest proportion of firms that perceive transportation to be a major or very severe problem to doing business is in the north (43 percent), followed by the center-west (33 percent). In contrast, only 13 percent of firms in the northeast and the south consider transportation to be a major or very severe constraint on their operations. Such results suggest that the supply of transportation services has not yet caught up with the demand of regional producers.

Firms in India also are seriously constrained by the quality of the country's physical infrastructure and, particularly, by the unreliability and high cost of electricity. Power supply is the most problematic element, with a third of busi-

---

13. A billion is 1,000 million.

14. These losses reflect not just the quality of roads and the vehicle fleet of the trucking industry but also the security situation and the prevalence of crime in different regions.

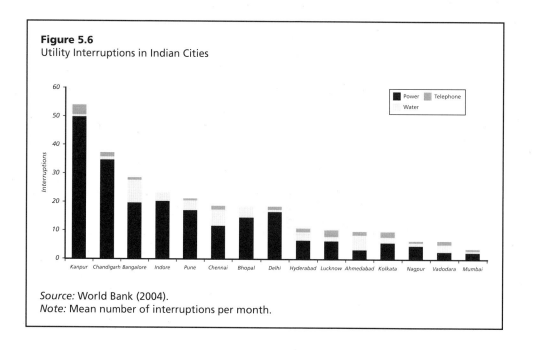

Figure 5.6
Utility Interruptions in Indian Cities

Source: World Bank (2004).
Note: Mean number of interruptions per month.

nesses rating it as a major or severe bottleneck.[15] By way of comparison, only 13 percent of respondents cite transport as a problem. Indian manufacturers face an average of 17 significant power outages per month, which, through downtime and damage to materials-in-process and equipment, collectively cost firms nearly a tenth of the total value of output. Power supply disruptions are especially frequent in Bangalore, Chandigarh, Delhi, Indore, and Kanpur, while Ahmedabad, Mumbai, and Vadodara experience relatively few outages (see figure 5.6).

It also takes new firms in India significantly longer than their peers in other major developing countries to obtain a connection to the public grid (World Bank 2004). On average, the wait is some 6.5 weeks, compared to three weeks in China or 1.5 weeks in Brazil. To cope with power outages and connection delays, more than three-fifths of Indian manufacturing firms own generators (see figure 5.7).[16] The figure is substantially higher in major industrial centers such as Delhi, Hyderabad, Chennai, and Bangalore, where firms rely on private generation for between 15 and 20 percent of their electricity needs. Although the proportion of business running generators decreased substantially by 2006, as assessed in the 2006 ICS, the share of own-generated electricity actually went up both over the full sample and across state groups, which is consistent with the fact that the proportion of businesses rating power shortages as a growth constraint did not fall between the two surveys.

---

15. In the 2006 ICS, electricity supply is the most frequently cited constraint to the ease of doing business, at 36 percent, an increase from 29 percent in 2003.

16. This compares to 20 percent in Malaysia, 27 percent in China, and 17 percent in Brazil.

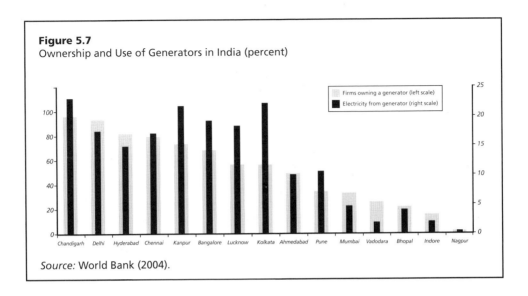

Figure 5.7
Ownership and Use of Generators in India (percent)

Source: World Bank (2004).

Overall, India's combined real cost of power is 74 percent higher than Malaysia's and 39 percent higher than China's.[17] It is estimated that reliable, affordable energy would increase the productivity of manufacturing labor by more than 80 percent in high-cost cities.

Although generation capacities in India are generally considered sufficient to meet the country's needs, there has been serious underinvestment over the years in transmission and distribution infrastructure. In addition, many of India's state electricity boards have long maintained a deliberate policy of cross-subsidizing the supply of electricity to households and agricultural producers by charging excessive tariffs to industry. This, and the boards' growing failure to protect transmission and collect bills, has led to serious underinvestment in maintenance and capacity. India has recently made efforts to attract private investment in generation and distribution, but these efforts have yet to bear fruit, partly due to the absence of a regulatory framework in which potential investors have confidence.

India's infrastructure is also severely deficient in the provision of transport services to industry (see World Bank 2004). India has no interstate expressways linking its major economic centers and only 3,000 kilometers of four-lane highways.[18] Just over half of India's roads are paved, and the average speed of trucks and buses on Indian highways is a paltry 30–40 kilometers an hour, owing to both congestion and the poor quality of road infrastructure. Although

---

17. India has significant interstate variations in power tariffs. For instance, Uttar Pradesh and Gujarat charge Rs6.64 and Rs4.39 per kilowatt hour, respectively, compared to Rs3.22 and Rs3.00 per kilowatt hour in Orissa and Punjab, respectively.

18. By way of comparison, China has built 25,000 kilometers of four- to six-lane, access-controlled expressways in the past 10 years.

Indian Railways is the second largest rail network in the world, the service is inefficient. The practice of cross-subsidizing passenger fares results in high cargo fares, while congestion along main lines results in unreliable long-haul delivery times.[19] Due to the obvious problems in Indian transport, the government has made the development of the road transport system an investment priority. The Golden Quadrilateral project and the North South-East West Highway project will help to reduce both the time and the cost of traveling between India's main centers. However, even assuming that these projects are completed on schedule by the end of 2008, reasonably well-surfaced, four-lane national highways will account for just 22 percent of India's national highways and none of the state highways.

In contrast, in South Africa losses due to power outages are modest, and the cost of power is low by international standards. Overall, manufacturing firms in South Africa lose less than 1 percent of output to electricity outages. As a result, less than 10 percent of South African firms see the need to own a generator.

As found with other aspects of the investment climate, infrastructure is a priority issue for two of these countries of focus. Of the three, India suffers the greatest problems with the quality of its physical infrastructure. Power supplies are extremely unreliable, due to inadequate transmission facilities, and the transportation infrastructure is primitive. However, some regions of Brazil also have serious infrastructural issues, with firms in the north and northeast losing significant portions of production due to power failures and firms in the center-west losing goods in transit due to inadequate transport infrastructure. South Africa is the exception, with comparatively few physical infrastructure limitations.

Cost and Availability of Skilled Labor

As firms attempt to increase the amount of value added during production and compete with firms overseas, the availability of skilled labor can be a crucial determinant of performance. Where it is difficult to find or hire such labor, market opportunities may go amiss and production runs may suffer disruption. Firms often pay excessive premiums for skilled workers, which is one factor that raises the costs of production and renders firms uncompetitive in the international market.

Given the importance of labor costs and availability of skills in the country, the South Africa investment climate assessment report explored in more depth the determinants of wages in the country (see World Bank 2007a). An econometric analysis controlling for myriad potential explanatory variables was per-

---

19. In a situation of zero cross-subsidization, the ratio of passenger earning per passenger kilometer to freight earning per metric ton of freight kilometer should be 1. For India, it is 0.3.

formed: firm size and sector to account for differences in monitoring costs and firm quality using foreign ownership, export status, age, age squared, and the share of workers with 10 or more years of schooling. It also includes the share of workers unionized as a measure of differences in the bargaining power as well as total factor productivity (TFP) to proxy for the size of available rents. The results for each job category are shown in columns 1–4 of table 5.2; the average firm wage is shown in column 5.

Table 5.2
Determinants of Wages in South Africa: A Firm-Level Estimation

Independent variable	Managers (1)	Professionals (2)	Skilled (3)	Unskilled (4)	Total (5)
50–99 employees	0.179 (0.062)**	-0.011 (0.116)	0.203 (0.088)*	0.142 (0.067)*	0.162 (0.103)
100–499 employees	0.253 (0.073)**	0.175 (0.127)	0.084 (0.161)	0.263 (0.075)**	0.217 (0.120)
More than 500 employees	0.370 (0.075)**	0.140 (0.159)	0.279 (0.118)*	0.321 (0.092)**	0.190 (0.127)
Firm exports greater than 10 percent of sales	0.139 (0.055)*	0.098 (0.112)	–0.048 (0.161)	0.082 (0.067)	0.225 (0.121)
Firm foreign-owned	0.040 (0.057)	–0.056 (0.119)	0.081 (0.116)	0.017 (0.080)	0.125 (0.101)
Firm age	0.055 (0.019)**	0.102 (0.050)*	0.089 (0.040)*	0.045 (0.035)	–0.041 (0.042)
Firm age squared	–0.001 (0.000)**	–0.001 (0.001)	–0.001 (0.000)*	–0.001 (0.000)	0.000 (0.000)
Percent of workers with 6–9 years of schooling	0.002 (0.002)	0.004 (0.002)	0.003 (0.002)	0.001 (0.002)	–0.004 (0.003)
Percent of workers with 10–12 years of schooling	0.003 (0.001)*	0.003 (0.003)	0.001 (0.002)	0.004 (0.002)**	0.002 (0.002)
Percent of workers with more than 12 years of schooling	0.004 (0.002)	–0.003 (0.004)	0.015 (0.003)**	0.003 (0.003)	0.008 (0.003)**
Percent of workers who are unionized	0.001 (0.001)	0.000 (0.002)	0.003 (0.001)*	0.002 (0.001)	–0.001 (0.001)
Constant	7.973 (0.413)**	6.666 (0.981)**	6.612 (0.846)**	6.280 (0.645)**	9.728 (0.893)**
Observations	315	193	309	296	386
R^2	0.25	0.19	0.20	0.23	0.12
F test firm size matters	8.34	1.45	2.86	5.50	1.35
Prob > F	0.00	0.23	0.04	0.00	0.26

Source: World Bank (2007a).
Note: Robust standard errors are in parenthesis. Dependent variable is Log (average monthly wage in thousands of rand).
* Significant at 5 percent.
** Significant at 1 percent.

Firm size explains a significant proportion of variation in average monthly wages for managers, skilled workers, and unskilled production workers.[20] Holding all other factors constant, a manager in a medium-size firm (50–99 employees) earns about 18 percent more than a manager in a firm with fewer than 50 employees. The wage gap is much larger for very large firms, with managers earning nearly 40 percent more. This wage–firm size profile is also apparent in the determination of unskilled wages: an unskilled worker in very large, large, and medium firms earns 32, 26, and 14 percent more, respectively, than an unskilled worker in a small firm.

The relationship between firm size and average wages is consistent with the efficiency wage theory, which predicts higher wages as monitoring costs rise. Holding everything else constant, large and very large firms pay an additional 700–900 rand per month for an unskilled worker than small firms pay. Although unobservable differences in worker quality cannot be ruled out, it is unlikely that these differences can account for a 25–30 percent difference in the average monthly wage for an unskilled worker.

Results suggest strong effects of productivity on wages. TFP is also included to test for the sensitivity of wages to profitability. The effect is strongest for skilled workers: a 1 percent increase in the firm's productivity is associated with a 0.7, 0.95, 1.8, and 0.7 percent increase in monthly wages for managers, professionals, skilled, and unskilled workers, respectively.

Measures of firm quality are also associated with higher wages. Exporting firms pay 14 percent higher wages to managers, ceteris paribus. Similarly, older firms pay higher wages to managers and skilled workers. The association between firm quality and wages can arise because workers with higher unobservable qualities match with better firms. The other reason could be that higher-quality firms are less likely to be liquidity constrained and can, therefore, afford to pay efficiency wages.

The availability of skills is the most commonly cited constraint on the operations and growth of firms in South Africa, with some 35.5 percent of managers surveyed regarding it as a "major" or "very severe" obstacle for their business (World Bank 2007a).[21] Consistent with such perceptions, skilled workers attract an extremely high premium in South Africa: an additional year of education in South Africa is associated with an 11–12 percent increase in wages, compared with 5–7 percent in most developed economies (see table 5.3). This is further reflected in a high level of wage inequality in South African industry. While the median monthly wage for an unskilled production worker in South Africa is about $241 (in 2002), a manager in South Africa commands about $1,850 a month. Compare this to Brazil, where unskilled workers average about $167

---

20. The omitted category is small firms.

21. This compares to 33.5 percent for macroeconomic instability and 33 percent for labor regulations.

Table 5.3
Median Monthly Wages in Select Countries, by Type of Worker (in US$)

Country	Managers	Professionals	Skilled production workers	Unskilled production workers	Total
Brazil	542	568	241	167	224
China	128	120	72	76	131
South Africa	1,848	803	487	241	675
Poland	738	369	320	246	408

Source: World Bank (2007a).

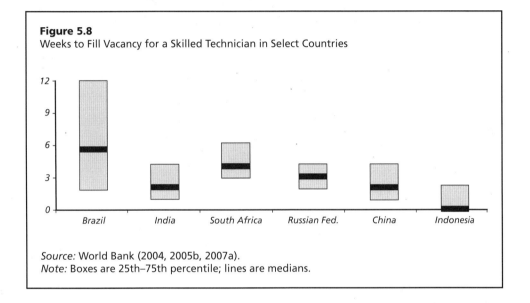

Figure 5.8
Weeks to Fill Vacancy for a Skilled Technician in Select Countries

Source: World Bank (2004, 2005b, 2007a).
Note: Boxes are 25th–75th percentile; lines are medians.

a month and managers average $542 a month. This translates into significant additional costs of production, which render South African firms uncompetitive relative to firms in other developing countries. South African firms also require a median time of four weeks to fill a skilled vacancy, compared to just two weeks in China and India (see figure 5.8). In Brazil, however, firms require a median of nearly six weeks to fill a skilled vacancy, and some 25 percent of hiring firms report spending 12 weeks or longer.

Despite the concerns that South African managers express about the availability of skills, relatively few firms in South Africa have training programs (see table 5.4). As noted in the investment climate assessment, while around four out of five workers in Brazil, China, and Poland undergo firm-level training programs, less than half of South African firms offer such training. The figure is also low in India, where 55 percent of skilled workers and only a third of unskilled workers receive training.

Table 5.4
Frequency of Firm-based Training in Select Countries

Country	Skilled workers	Unskilled workers
Brazil	77	68
Poland	80	86
India	55	33
China	69	63
South Africa	45	46

Source: World Bank (2007a).

Firms in South Africa have to pay significantly more to hire skilled workers than firms in other developing countries with which they compete. South African firms also spend longer looking for skilled workers to hire than their competitors in other countries. The time to fill a skilled vacancy is even more problematic in Brazil, however. In both of these respects, India seems to perform particularly well, although finding available skilled labor is becoming increasingly difficult in India; in some sectors, such as information technology and consulting, shortages of skilled labor are beginning to prompt wage spirals in an effort to attract foreign-based workers, even from the United States. In summary, cost and availability of skilled labor, while currently the most significant problem cited in South Africa, are an issue that all three countries need to address.

Crime

The incidence of crime can add significantly to the costs of doing business, both directly through the loss of plant equipment and produce to vandalism or theft and indirectly through the cost of employing security agencies to protect the firm's property.

Crime is rarely cited as a major constraint by Indian firms.[22] However, it is a pressing problem for businesses in Brazil and South Africa, where managers express particular concern about the effect of lawlessness on their ability to conduct business. More than half of Brazilian managers, for instance, rate it as a "major" or "very severe" constraint. In South Africa, crime ranks fourth overall among concerns of managers, cited by just under 30 percent of respondents. Objective indicators show that Brazil and South Africa are representative of countries where crime and security are considered important, though not critical, problems. Nevertheless, compared to other emerging economies, the

---

22. Crime is cited even less in the 2006 ICS than the 2003 survey and is not among the leading group of constraints in either year.

security environment harms competitiveness and makes Brazil and South Africa less attractive destinations for foreign investment.

In the ICS, approximately 23 percent of Brazilian managers reported that their firm had suffered losses due to arson, theft, or vandalism in 2002 that averaged 0.58 percent of their total sales. Results from a follow-up survey with about 440 Brazilian firms conducted in 2005 show that such losses had increased in all regions except the northeast, representing losses ranging from 0.95 percent of total sales in the northeast region to a full 2 percent in the metropolitan region of São Paolo. In addition, some 81 percent of Brazilian firms surveyed in 2002 reported that they had to incur additional costs for security (World Bank 2007e).

Such costs seem to be lower than those experienced by firms elsewhere in Latin America (see table 5.5). Three-quarters of Peruvian firms, for instance, have experienced direct costs from crime. Within Brazil, firms in the north seem to bear the highest direct costs of criminal sales, averaging some 1.5 percent of annual sales.[23] Security costs and the costs of prevention are highest in the center-west, which is also the region with the highest value of consignment cargo lost during transport, and the high costs of security possibly reflect firms' need to secure cargo in transit. Security costs are lowest in the south of Brazil.

As detailed in the investment climate assessment, the incidence of property crime in South Africa has increased markedly since 1994, and this has raised the costs of doing business (see World Bank 2007a).[24] More than half of South African firms reported direct costs as a result of arson, theft, or vandalism in the

Table 5.5
Percent of Firms Experiencing Crime and Incurring Security Costs in Select Countries

Country	Incidence of crime in past year	Incidence of extra security costs
Brazil	23	81
Ecuador	37	93
Peru	74	66
India	—	73
China	10	48
Pakistan	8	59
South Africa	53	81
Kenya	35	92
Senegal	42	76

Source: World Bank (2004, 2005b, 2007a).
— Not available.

23. Concern over crime is particularly high in the center-west and southeast, where it is cited by 56 and 58 percent of respondents, respectively. Firms in the north and northeast are less concerned, with only 32 and 44 percent of firms, respectively, citing crime as a problem.

24. Between 1994 and 2000, common robbery increased 168 percent, and aggravated robbery increased 31 percent.

past year, and four out of five firms reported incurring extra costs for securing their property. The incidence of direct losses to crime, although not particularly unusual for firms in Africa, is nonetheless significantly higher in South Africa than in Kenya or Senegal. Direct losses account for a third of the total costs of crime, which is more than in most countries and suggests that the means by which firms protect themselves from crime are less effective in South Africa than in other countries. Although the reporting of crime to the police is relatively high in South Africa (58 percent), nearly three-quarters of firms indicate that none of the incidents reported has been solved. The burden of crime is not distributed evenly across firms. In general, manufacturing firms face fewer losses than firms involved in retail and wholesale trade or construction.[25] Large firms also tend to face higher losses than smaller firms. After controlling for other factors, firms in Durban face the heaviest losses, while firms in Johannesburg face relatively modest losses.

Brazil and South Africa have a reputation for being especially afflicted with violent crime, and it is a clear concern to the business community.[26] The data collected through the investment climate surveys, however, indicate that, while Brazilian and South African firms incur quantifiable costs from crime, both directly and indirectly, the incidence of crime in both countries is not unusually high compared with the rest of the region.

---

25. About 52 percent of manufacturing firms experienced losses from crime in 2003, compared to 54 percent of construction firms and 64 percent of wholesale-retail firms.

26. In February 2007, President Lula da Silva spoke out on the plague of violence but emphasized the need to invest in jobs and education to reduce the problem. Brazil has the fourth highest murder rate in the world, and murder rates in small Brazilian towns exceed those in big cities, according to the Organization of Iberoamerican States. In South Africa, the business community even resorted to newspaper advertisements calling on the government to do more to tackle crime in early 2007. "Brazil's Lula Says No Quick Fix for Rising Violence," Reuters News, February 28, 2007; "Mbeki Faces Flak from South African Business over Crime Rate," Agence France Presse, February 6, 2007.

6

Potential Reforms and Their Estimated Effects

In this chapter we consider the impact of sample potential reforms that could be undertaken at the national level and provide evidence of their possible effects. We begin with an exercise examining the impacts on productivity of potential improvements in investment climate variables, followed by an example of the potential benefits of improved access to finance.

Investment Climate Reform and Productivity

As discussed in earlier chapters, economic theory posits that improvements in investment climate indicators are associated with increases in the ability of firms to employ available inputs to produce marketable goods and services. In this chapter we use firm-level data from the investment climate survey to investigate how investment climate variables affect the productivity of firms in different sectors across Brazil, India, and South Africa. To evaluate the impact of investment climate variables on productivity at the firm level, we follow the one-step regression approach by Escribano and Guasch (2005). Similar attempts to estimate the productivity impact of investment climate variables have been undertaken by using different statistical estimation techniques. Dollar, Hallward-Driemeier, and Mengistae (2004), for instance, have studied investment climate effects on total factor productivity (TFP) using a two-step estimation procedure.

Due to data limitations, it was not possible to focus specifically on top constraints cited for each country, such as corruption or skilled labor; instead, related variables were chosen, where feasible. The analysis therefore focuses specifically on the relationship between firm-level productivity and the following investment climate variables: number of days taken to clear imports and exports

Table 6.1
Regression of Firm-level Productivity on Select Productivity Indicators

Indicator	Regression results
Efficiency of customs procedures	0.0144
	(0.3)
Burden of inspections	–0.1264
	(–1.9)
Losses due to power outages	–0.0985
	(–1.57)
Capacity utilization	0.0033
	(4.45)
Use of computer	0.0027
	(3.97)
Ownership of generator	0.0888
	(4.69)
Internet access	0.1189
	(1.94)
Training	0.0205
	(0.82)
Research and development	0.0058
	(0.86)
Foreign ownership	0.0245
	(0.99)
Public listing	0.0537
	(1.28)
Age	–0.0139
	(–1.08)
Number of observations	2,057
R^2	0.96

Source: Author's calculations based on World Bank ICS Brazil (2003), ICS India (2003), and ICS South Africa (2004).

through customs; percent of sales lost due to power outages; ownership of a generator; and the use of e-mail or Web sites in business; total number of days spent by managers with officials from regulatory agencies; percent of the work force that regularly uses a computer.[1] The results of the regression analysis are presented in table 6.1.

Across firms in the three countries, the results indicate a statistically significant relationship between firm-level productivity and ownership of an electrical generator, the burden of inspections, the regular use of a computer by the work force, and the use of e-mail or the Internet in the business.[2] Specifically, a 1

---

1. These variables are conditioned on capacity utilization, operation of training programs, spending on research and development, foreign ownership, public listing, and age of the firm. The specification follows the one-step regression approach of Escribano and Guasch (2005: 23–24, 29–31, 47), with a Cobb-Douglas functional form with coefficients unrestricted at the country-industry level. Standard errors are clustered at the country-industry level.

2. The control variables found to be significant are capacity utilization and the natural log of the number of employees.

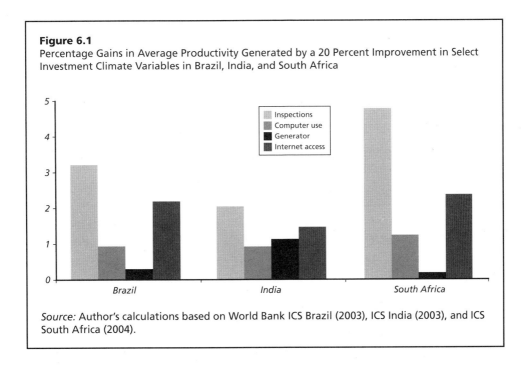

Figure 6.1
Percentage Gains in Average Productivity Generated by a 20 Percent Improvement in Select Investment Climate Variables in Brazil, India, and South Africa

Source: Author's calculations based on World Bank ICS Brazil (2003), ICS India (2003), and ICS South Africa (2004).

percent increase in ownership of an electrical generator is associated with a 0.09 percent increase in productivity, a 1 percent increase in the average number of days spent by managers with officials from regulatory agencies is associated with a 0.13 percent reduction in average firm-level productivity, a 1 percent increase in the percentage of the work force that regularly uses a computer is associated with a 0.003 percent increase in average firm-level productivity, and a 1 percent increase in access to the Internet and e-mail is associated with a 0.12 percent increase in productivity.

However, due to differences in these variables from one country to the next, firms in different countries are affected differently by changes in the investment climate. To examine this further, we simulate the effect on firm-level productivity of a 20 percent improvement in the four significant investment climate indicators identified for each of the three countries (see figure 6.1).

As registered by investment climate surveys, the lack of an inexpensive and reliable electricity supply is a common complaint among managers in India, with 29 percent of managers ranking electricity as a major constraint on the operation of their business. These indicators are supported by evidence that manufacturers face an average of 17 significant power outages per month. It is not surprising, therefore, that the effect of generator ownership on productivity is most pronounced in India. According to the simulation exercises, a 20 percent increase in the ownership of a generator would increase the productivity of firms in India 1.12 percent. As expected, the effects of such increases in Brazil and South Africa would be less pronounced: 0.30 and 0.17 percent, respectively.

The effect of worksite inspections by regulatory agencies is found to have a disproportionately large impact on firm-level productivity in all three countries. However, the burden of inspections has a particularly detrimental effect in South Africa, a moderate effect in Brazil, and a smaller, but still significant, effect in India. In South Africa, for instance, a 20 percent fall in the incidence of worksite inspections would increase firm productivity 4.74 percent, on average. In Brazil the estimated effect would be a 3.19 increase, while in India it would be 2.03 percent. These results are somewhat surprising given that, of the three countries, firms in India spend the largest percentage of their time on regulation. In effect, the results reflect the high frequency of inspections in South Africa.

The use of information technology is an emerging issue for enterprises in the developing world, and the simulation predicts that productivity in all three countries would improve substantially if firms would make increasing use of computers, the Internet, and e-mail in their day-to-day operations. The anticipated impact on productivity of an increase in computer use is relatively even across the three countries: a 20 percent improvement in the number of employees using computers would raise productivity 0.94 percent in Brazil, 0.92 percent in India, and 1.22 percent in South Africa. The effect of Internet access on productivity is roughly double the effect of the simple use of computers, although this is less pronounced in India than in Brazil and South Africa. In Brazil the anticipated effect of a 20 percent increase in the proportion of firms using the Internet or e-mail to contact clients or suppliers would be 2.20 percent. In India and South Africa the impact would be 1.44 and 2.34 percent, respectively.

The results of these simulations can help to guide country governments in targeting reforms to the areas of greatest impact. While the results are preliminary, they indicate that firm-level productivity in all three countries would benefit significantly from a reduction in the frequency of inspections and an improvement in Internet access. Reducing the frequency of inspections is a clear priority for both Brazil and South Africa, and improving the reliability of the electricity supply would raise productivity significantly in India.

As new data become available, it should be possible to explore further the impacts on productivity of other constraints. Policy makers might benefit, for example, from seeing productivity impacts broken down by firm characteristics, such as size or sector, for example, focusing on the impacts on exporting firms.

Examining Options for Microeconomic Reform: Access to Credit

As noted in chapter 5, access to finance is a major problem for firms in both Brazil and India. In Brazil, three-quarters of managers cite the cost of finance as a constraint on the growth of their business, which is not surprising given median nominal interest rates of around 40 percent. The problems in India relate

Table 6.2

Credit Information in Brazil, India, and South Africa

Question	Brazil	India	South Africa
Are both individuals and firms listed in credit registry?	Yes	No	Yes
Are both positive and negative data distributed?	Yes	Yes	Yes
Does the registry collect credit information from financial institutions as well as retailers and utility providers?	Yes	No	Yes
Are more than two years of historical credit information available for distribution?	No	Yes	Yes
Are data on all loans larger than 1 percent of income per capita recorded?	Yes	Yes	Yes
Is it guaranteed by law that borrowers can inspect their data?	Yes	No	No

Source: World Bank (2006a); http://www.doingbusiness.org/

as much to access as to cost. The absence of reliable credit information is a particular problem, hampering the extension of credit to small- and medium-size enterprises (see table 6.2).

The impediments to efficient credit markets differ significantly between countries, and, as such, reformers need to develop policies that address conditions specific to local conditions. Nevertheless, economic theory and cross-country evidence underscore the general importance of creditor rights and the availability of credit information in the development of private credit markets. Creditor rights are important because lenders are likely to be more willing to extend credit in environments where they are able to force repayment, seize collateral, or even gain control of the firm (Djankov, McLiesh, and Shleifer 2007; see table 6.3). Information on borrowers, their credit history, or other lenders provides a mechanism through which potential lenders can assess risk and adjust costs accordingly, enabling a more efficient credit market.

Djankov, McLiesh, and Shleifer (2007) examine the quantitative relationship between the development of credit markets and creditor rights and the availability of credit information for 129 countries between 1978 and 2005. Their index of credit rights quantifies four powers of secured lenders in bankruptcy: (a) whether there are restrictions, such as creditor consent, when a debtor files for reorganization; (b) whether secured creditors are able to seize their collateral after reorganization is approved; (c) whether secured creditors are given priority to the proceeds of liquidation; and (d) whether an administrator is responsible for running the business during the reorganization. The availability of information on the standing of borrowers in the financial system is given by the existence of a public credit registry, maintained by a government agency mandated to collect information on the standing of borrowers in the financial system, or a private credit information bureau operated by a private firm or nonprofit organization (see table 6.4).

Table 6.3

Collateral and Bankruptcy Laws in Brazil, India, and South Africa

Question	Brazil	India	South Africa
Does the law allow all natural and legal persons to be party to collateral agreements?	No	Yes	No
Does the law allow for general description of assets, so that all types of assets can be used as collateral?	No	No	No
Does the law allow for general description of debt, so that all types of obligations can be secured?	Yes	Yes	Yes
Does a unified registry exist for all security rights in movable property?	No	No	No
Do secured creditors have absolute priority to their collateral outside bankruptcy procedures?	Yes	No	Yes
Do secured creditors have absolute priority to their collateral in bankruptcy procedures?	No	No	Yes
During reorganization, are secured creditors' claims exempt from an automatic stay on enforcement?	No	Yes	No
During reorganization, is management's control of the company's assets suspended?	No	Yes	Yes
Does the law authorize parties to agree on out-of-court enforcement?	No	Yes	Yes
May parties have recourse to out-of-court enforcement without restrictions?	No	No	No

Source: World Bank (2006a); http://www.doingbusiness.org/

Table 6.4

Share of Adults Covered by Credit Information Registries in Brazil, India, and South Africa, 2006
(percent)

Type of coverage	Brazil	India	South Africa
Public registry	9.2	0.0	0.0
Private bureau	43.0	6.1	53.0

Source: World Bank (2006a); http://www.doingbusiness.org/

Djankov, McLiesh, and Shleifer (2007) find that countries with stronger legal protection have deeper credit markets than countries with weaker legal protection.[3] The legal authority of secured creditors to grab and liquidate collateral through the absence of an automatic stay on assets and respect for the priority of secured creditors are found to be important determinants of market depth, while restrictions on entering reorganization and mandatory removal of management are less important. With regard to sources of credit information, they note a positive conditional correlation between public registries and credit depth in poorer countries and between private credit registries and credit depth

---

3.   Specifically, they find that when the creditor rights index rises by 1, the ratio of private credit to GDP rises 0.06.

in richer countries. In the poorer countries, where private credit registries are uncommon for reasons of cost or compliance, governments have a constructive role to play in maintaining public credit registries.

In order to examine how reforms might affect the depth of the financial sector in Brazil, India, and South Africa, we use cross-country time-series data from Djankov, McLiesh, and Shleifer (2007) and the 2006 World Development indicators to build a model of the relationship between financial sector institutions and the ratio of private credit to GDP.[4] Similar to the findings of Djankov, McLiesh, and Shleifer (2007), within the full sample of 129 countries, depth of private credit is found to be statistically and quantitatively related to the strength of creditor rights and the operation of a private credit information bureau.[5] Specifically, reforms to improve the rights of secured creditors are associated with ratios of private credit to GDP that are higher by an average of 6.3 percent, while the operation of private credit information bureaus is associated with ratios of private credit to GDP that are higher by an average of 12.6 percent.

The clear lesson for policy makers in Brazil, India, and South Africa is that stronger creditor rights and expanded coverage of credit information registries would improve access to credit.

---

4. We use a Prais-Winsten correlated panels corrected standard errors model assuming first-order autocorrelation in which the coefficient of the AR(1) process is specific to each panel and corrected using a time-series autocorrelation correction. The dependent variable is the logarithm of the average of the ratio of private credit to GDP in the five years subsequent to the year in which the independent variables are observed. The independent variables of interest are (1) five-point measure of creditor rights from Djankov, McLiesh, and Shleifer (2007), (2) dummy variable for the existence of a public credit registry in the country-year, and (3) dummy variable for the existence of a private credit information bureau in the country-year. In addition, we add the following control variables: (a) logarithm of gross national income in current U.S. dollars, (b) annual GDP growth, (c) logarithm of annual percentage inflation (GDP deflator), and (d) the dependent variable lagged by five years. The addition of the control variables follows Djankov, McLiesh, and Shleifer (2007), who posit that larger economies may have larger credit markets because of economies of scale in organizing the supporting institutions, that rapid economic expansion may require more credit, and that inflation may devalue the stock of outstanding debt or otherwise undermine debt contracting.

5. The full sample covers 128 countries between 1978 and 2005, comprising 1,909 observations. Coefficients on both creditor rights and the dummy variable for the operation of a private credit information bureau have p scores of 0.000. Coefficients on all the control variables are significant except GDP growth. The coefficient on the dummy variable for the operation of a public credit bureau has a positive sign, but is highly insignificant. The R^2 is 0.9561.

7
Lessons from
Country Experience

Brazil, India, and South Africa have initiated reforms in recent years to improve their investment climate. While offering insight on how to overcome technical challenges, these efforts offer especially valuable lessons for the management of reform. Managing reform is crucial, as investment climate reforms are difficult to initiate, implement, and sustain. Many reformers struggle with identifying priorities for reform, which is one of the biggest challenges in the early stages. Others have difficulty overcoming opposition from interest groups, delivering the expected results, or sustaining reform efforts in the long run.

This chapter provides case studies of reforms in Brazil, India, and South Africa. The studies are relevant for emerging economies that are considering undertaking investment climate reforms. Clearly there is no standard process for reforms, and many of the circumstances described in the case studies are specific to the individual countries. Yet valuable lessons have emerged during the restructuring process, and highlighting these is intended to offer guidance to reformers undertaking similar challenges in other countries. The cases may even be of interest to policy makers within the country studied, given that the lessons of reform, particularly regarding process, may be applicable to more than one area of the investment climate.

The case studies developed were selected in coordination with the World Bank teams from Brazil, India, and South Africa based on their potential to offer practical suggestions for the management of reform in those and other emerging economies. Therefore, they do not necessarily correspond with the issues cited most frequently as major obstacles or the areas of best performance for each country. The cases address issues such as tax policy, formalization, innovation, and skilled labor, that are relevant in many countries. Each case study addresses a different aspect of the investment climate and the impacts of government policy.

For each, we examine the context for reform and the push to initiate change, detail the implementation process, and assess the impact of the reform and how reform measures were sustained, and even broadened, over time.

The following cases are featured. The case study of Brazil's SIMPLES reform shows how investment climate reformers can target a specific segment of the economy, in this case micro and small firms. The case study of India's software sector highlights the importance of sector reforms as a catalyst for economic growth and the need for continuous oversight and efforts to sustain the impacts of both sector reforms and investment climate reforms in general. The case study of South Africa's corporate tax system shows the importance of taking sustained steps in a predictable manner to reduce policy uncertainty and establish trust. Finally, the case of the Accelerated and Shared Growth Initiative for South Africa (ASGISA) considers how a government, and other interested stakeholders, can use available data and tools to pinpoint priorities for reform that support a broader process of reform. This case describes how detailed diagnostics and analytical frameworks can help to identify priorities and build support for continued reform.

A Flat Tax for Micro and Small Firms: The SIMPLES Reform in Brazil

One of the most important microeconomic reforms implemented in Brazil in the last 10 years is the introduction of a simplified tax regime for micro and small enterprises (MSEs). The overhaul of the tax regime was aimed at making the tax burden on MSEs more manageable, encouraging small businesses to participate in the tax system, and creating jobs in the formal sector. The main reforms were introduced in 1996 with the creation of an integrated system for collecting tax revenue from MSEs, and the process has continued since then, including the approval in 2006 of Complementary Law no. 123/2006, which establishes an MSE statute.

This case study analyzes how the Brazilian government managed to reform the tax system for MSEs. It highlights the main characteristics of the reform as well as its impacts on the generation of formal employment and the streamlining of business. It concludes with some conjectures about the possible extension of the reform.

The Context of Reform

Brazil has a complex tax structure with many types of taxes, and firms find it hard to comply with the onerous tax regulations. The high level of taxation (taxes are imposed on different bases) and the federalist structure of the country (the three levels of government each impose taxes) are the key reasons for this complexity. Brazil has four value added taxes alone: one at the state level and three at the federal level. Moreover, payroll taxes represent 35 percent of the total tax burden imposed on firms. However, the tax "wedge" that exists between the take-home pay and the wage paid by employers is around 65 percent, placing a heavy load on the hiring of workers.[1] This fact contributes to a high level of informality (more than 50 percent of the labor force is either self-employed or salaried but not registered). This situation has been aggravated by a substantial rise in the tax burden: the government has been increasing taxes in an effort to combine fiscal discipline with rigid and growing levels of current spending (see figure 7.1).

In the 1990s the government faced growing pressures to implement tax reform. Recognizing that the current policy was actually losing revenue as a result of the extensive informal labor force, the authorities proposed an initiative to reduce the cost of doing business for MSEs. This 1996 legislation (Law no. 9,317/1996) consolidated the special tax rules applying to MSEs in order to facilitate tax payments and broaden the tax base.

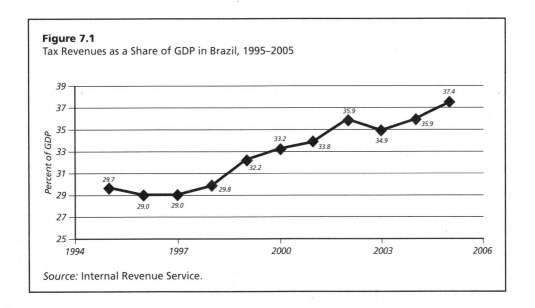

Figure 7.1
Tax Revenues as a Share of GDP in Brazil, 1995–2005

Source: Internal Revenue Service.

---

1. World Bank (2002). For example, the tax "wedge" in the United States, Germany, France, and Sweden (the heaviest among OECD countries) is around 18, 32, 39, and 42 percent, respectively.

Implementing the Reform

The SIMPLES was the first attempt to standardize the tax treatment given to MSEs in Brazil. The system establishes the procedures for tax incidence and tax revenue collection by the federal government, with the possibility of consolidating these procedures with those at the state and municipal levels. Six distinct federal taxes were consolidated under the SIMPLES. If state and municipalities also join the process, then their state sales tax and municipal tax on services are also incorporated in the simplified system.[2] However, firms using the SIMPLES are still required to pay other federal taxes based on the general principles governing each of them.

To determine eligibility for the simplified system, MSEs are grouped according to their annual gross revenues, with new categories established by Law no. 9,732/1998 and Law no. 11,307/2006.[3] Within each group, subgroups were created in order to establish a progressive tax rate system (see table 7.1). Qualifying businesses using the SIMPLES system can substitute up to eight taxes for a single tax rate on their annual gross revenues. For businesses eligible to use the SIMPLES for tax payments, the changes associated with implementation of the system are detailed in table 7.2.

---

2.   The six taxes are (1) business federal tax responsibilities (IRPJ, Imposto de Renda Pessoa Jurídica), (2) social contributions on net profits (CSLL, Contribuição Social sobre o Lucro Líquido), (3) social financial contributions (Cofins, Contribuição Financeira Social), (4) the Social Integration Program (PIS, Programa de Integração Social) and the Asset-Building Program for Public Workers (Pasep, Programa de Formação do Patrimônio do Servidor Público), (5) federal taxes, including social security (INSS), and (6) the tax on manufactured goods (IPI, Imposto sobre Produtos Industrializados). The state sales tax is the ICMS (Imposto de Circulação de Mercadorias e Serviços); the municipal tax on services is the ISS (Imposto sobre Serviços).

3.   In Brazil, the Statute of the Small and Micro Enterprises and the SIMPLES adopt the criterion based on the firm's annual gross revenues to classify firms according to their size. A firm is considered micro if its annual gross revenues are equal to or less than R$240,000 and is considered small if its annual gross revenues are between R$240,001 and R$2.4 million. Nevertheless, it is important to remember that the SIMPLES does not apply to the whole universe of SMEs; it only applies to some economic sectors, as described in the law. Firms in banking, credit, insurance, real estate, storage, marketing, factoring, cleaning, and private security are not eligible to participate in the reformed system. However, most government institutions (such as the Ministry of Employment) and those that provide business services to the private sector (such as SEBRAE) use employment to classify firms as small, medium, or large enterprises. MSEs are firms with gross revenues equal to or less than R$1.2 million in 2002. Medium and large firms are those with gross revenues higher than R$1.2 million in 2002. Therefore, the size classification of firms using the SIMPLES methodology was developed for the single purpose of tax revenues, while the usual classification takes into account the size of the firm's work force. This can be important to know given that other countries are unlikely to select the same revenue groupings, which must be appropriate to the local economy.

Table 7.1

SIMPLES: Tax Rates per Annual Gross Revenues for Micro and Small Enterprises (percent)

Firm size in R$; tax rates in percentages

Size of enterprise	IRPJ	CSLL	Confins	PIS/Pasep	INSS	IPI	ICMS/ISS	Total
Microenterprises								
≤ R$60,000	0.00	0.30	0.90	0.00	1.80	0.50	1.00	4.50
R$60,001–R$90,000	0.00	0.40	1.20	0.00	2.40	0.50	1.00	5.50
R$90,001–R$120,000	0.00	0.50	1.50	0.00	3.00	0.50	1.00	6.50
R$12,001–R$240,000	0.00	0.54	1.62	0.00	3.24	0.50	1.00	5.90
Small enterprises								
R$240,001–R$360,000	0.41	0.41	1.21	0.29	3.48	0.50	2.50	8.80
R$360,001–R$480,000	0.44	0.44	1.29	0.31	3.72	0.50	2.50	9.20
R$480,001–R$600,000	0.46	0.46	1.38	0.34	3.96	0.50	2.50	9.60
R$600,001–R$840,000	0.49	0.49	1.47	0.35	4.20	0.50	2.50	10.00
R$840,001–R$960,000	0.52	0.52	1.55	0.37	4.44	0.50	2.50	10.40
R$960,001– R$1,080,000	0.55	0.55	1.63	0.39	4.68	0.50	2.50	10.80
R$1,080,001–R$1,200,000	0.58	0.58	1.71	0.41	4.92	0.50	2.50	11.20
R$1,200,001–R$1,320,000	0.60	0.60	1.81	0.43	5.16	0.50	2.50	11.60
R$1,320,001–R$1,440,000	0.63	0.63	1.88	0.46	5.40	0.50	2.50	12.00
R$1,440,001–R$1,560,000	0.65	0.65	1.97	0.49	5.64	0.50	2.50	12.40
R$1,560,001–R$1,680,000	0.68	0.68	2.05	0.51	5.88	0.50	2.50	12.80
R$1,680,001–R$1,800,000	0.71	0.71	2.12	0.54	6.12	0.50	2.50	13.20
R$1,800,001–R$1,820,000	0.74	0.74	2.20	0.56	6.36	0.50	2.50	13.60
R$1,820,001–R$1,920,000	0.77	0.77	2.27	0.59	6.60	0.50	2.50	14.00
R$1,920,001–R$2,040,000	0.80	0.80	2.35	0.61	6.84	0.50	2.50	14.40
R$2,040,001–R$2,160,000	0.84	0.84	2.42	0.62	7.08	0.50	2.50	14.80
R$2,160,001–R$2,280,000	0.86	0.86	2.52	0.64	7.32	0.50	2.50	15.20
R$2,280,001–R$2,400,000	0.89	0.89	2.61	0.65	7.56	0.50	2.50	15.60

Source: Law no. 9,317/1996, changed by Law no. 9,732/1998, Law no. 10,256/2000, Law no. 11,196/2005, and Law no. 11,307/2006.

Note: Gross revenues are in *reales*. The first grouping consists of the first five taxes: IRPJ (business federal tax), CSLL (social contributions on net profits), Confins (social financial contributions), PIS/Pasep (the Social Integration Program and the Asset-Building Program for Public Workers), and INSS (social security tax). The second consists of the first group plus IPI (tax on manufactured goods). The third consists of the second group plus ICMS/ISS (state sales tax and municipal tax on services).

  a. Tax rate when firm pays IPI.

  b. Maximum rate when firm pays ICMS/ISS.

  c. Maximum total tax rate.

Table 7.2

Tax on MSEs in Brazil before and after the Implementation of SIMPLES
(percent of annual gross revenues unless otherwise noted)

Tax	Before SIMPLES		After SIMPLES	
	Micro	*Small*	*Micro*	*Small*
IRPJ	0.00	1.20	0.00	0.41–0.89
CSLL	0.96	1.44	0.30–0.54	0.41–0.89
Confins	2.00	3.00	0.90–1.62	1.21–2.61
PIS/Pasep	0.00	0.65	0.00	0.29–0.65
INSS	20.00[a]	20.00[a]	1.80–3.24	3.48–7.56
IPI	Varied	Varied	0.50	0.50
ICMS	Varied	Varied	Max 1.00	Max 2.50
ISS	Varied	Varied	Max 1.00	Max 2.50

Source: Internal Revenue Service.
a. Percent of payroll bill.

The Impacts of Reform

The introduction of the SIMPLES reform appears to have been successful in reducing informality in the Brazilian economy, measured as the share of registered
workers in the labor market and the number of licensed firms.

The flat tax introduced by the SIMPLES replaced most federal taxes, including social security. Prior to the SIMPLES, MSEs had to pay the INSS taxes
of 20 percent on the payroll bill. Under the new regime, INSS taxes vary between 1.80 and 3.24 percent of annual gross revenues for micro enterprises and
between 3.48 and 7.56 percent for small firms. Therefore, the formal hiring of
employees has ceased to be a significant additional tax cost for MSEs, encouraging formal employment.

Many micro and small enterprises have taken up the opportunities created by the SIMPLES legislation. Data from the Brazilian Ministry of Employment show that between 1995 and 1997, firms with 1–19 employees created
580,000 jobs in the formal sector.[4] Firms with more than 20 employees lost
about 420,000 jobs in the formal sector. Overall, 160,000 formal jobs were
added during 1995–97. For businesses located in Brazilian metropolitan areas,
informality in the labor market declined between 1997 and mid-1998, a result, in part, of the formalization of employment among MSEs (see figure 7.2).[5]

---

4.   Stock of workers as of December 31 for each fiscal year.
5.   In 2003 the second urban informal economy survey was conducted by the Brazilian Institute of
      Geography and Statistics, covering all the states and metropolitan areas in the country. Results
      show that there were 10.5 million small nonagricultural enterprises in Brazil. In comparison to
      the 1997 survey, there was an increase of 10 percent in the number of small enterprises, while
      the number of enterprises in the informal sector increased 9 percent, pointing to a smooth trend
      toward formalization.

Box 7.1 Estimating the Impact of SIMPLES on Formal Employment and Investment

Monteiro and Assunção (2006) employ a rigorous test to evaluate a sample of 40,000 firms located in Brazilian state capitals and metropolitan regions in order to assess the impact of simpler bureaucracy and lower taxes on the formality of firms and the consequences for investment. Using the enactment of SIMPLES as a source of exogenous reduction in the effective tax burden, they find an increase of 13 percentage points in licensing among firms in the retail sector. Using the launching of SIMPLES as an instrument for licensing, they find a positive and statistically significant effect of formality on the amount invested by retailers and a shift of such investments toward long-run projects. Moreover, the study highlights the obstacles that a heavy tax burden and time-consuming bureaucracy constitute for the regularization of retailers. The main results are reinforced in a propensity score-matching approach, which shows that the SIMPLES system not only increased the proportion of licensed firms in the retail sector but also was a valid instrument for licensing.

In a different exercise, Fajnzylber, Maloney, and Montes Rojas (2006) show that increases in formality driven by the SIMPLES reform are associated with increases in the use of paid labor and levels of capital intensity, accompanied by improvements in productivity. In particular, increases in the registration rate of micro firms that could be attributed to the new tax regime are associated with an estimated 5 percent increase in paid employment, a 15 percent boost in total factor productivity, and a 35 percent increase in labor productivity.

However, beyond this initial impact, the level of informality in the labor market continues to fluctuate. See box 7.1 for two exercises to determine the impact of SIMPLES on formal employment and investment.

The implementation of SIMPLES also significantly reduced the cost of administering the tax system. Given that the taxable income from MSEs is relatively low as a share of the taxable income for all firms, the SIMPLES reform was an important step toward rationalizing tax management for this group.[6] Simplification of the tax system for MSEs reduced both the number of tax forms and the length of the unified declaration (that is, the number of fields and pages) for MSEs and thus reduced the amount of information to be received and stored by the tax system administrator.[7] For fiscal year 2003, businesses using the SIMPLES system represented almost 70 percent of the total number of businesses filling out tax forms (see figure 7.3). Therefore, as the implementation of SIMPLES eased the oversight of MSEs, scarce labor resources at the Internal Revenue Services (Receita Federal) could be switched to supervising larger companies, optimizing the allocation of resources within the tax administrator.[8]

---

6. In 2004 total taxable income in Brazil was R$2.83 trillion, of which R$180 billion, or 6.1 percent, was from MSEs. In addition, MSEs report only 61 percent of their annual gross revenues for tax purposes (compared to 73 percent for medium and large enterprises).

7. Beginning in 2000, firms return the SIMPLES tax form to the administrator electronically.

8. It is also possible to consider that by simplifying the tax-filing process for MSEs, unintentional tax evasion is also curbed.

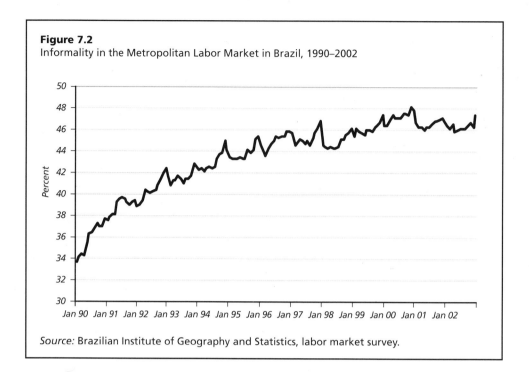

Figure 7.2
Informality in the Metropolitan Labor Market in Brazil, 1990–2002

Source: Brazilian Institute of Geography and Statistics, labor market survey.

In addition, the SIMPLES reform helped to improve the system of tax administration. The average number of federal fiscal inspections is significantly lower for MSEs (0.5 visit) than for medium and large firms (2.1 visits). Moreover, the average duration of each inspection is significantly lower among MSEs (3.4 hours) than among medium and large companies (7.9 hours). The tax administrator rejects many more tax forms among medium and large firms than among MSEs, which benefit from the simpler process made possible by the SIMPLES reforms.[9]

These improvements are reflected in the perceptions that MSEs have of the tax system.[10] MSEs are significantly less likely to report the following issues as major or severe constraints on their growth and operation: (a) the treatment given by the fiscal administration, (b) the filling out and return of tax forms, (c) the frequent changes of tax regulations, and (d) the efficacy of mechanisms with which to appeal tax-related matters (see figure 7.4).

9.   In the period 2000–02, the share of firms that had their tax forms rejected by the administrator was 3.1 for MSEs and 6.8 percent for medium and large firms.

10. The investment climate survey conducted in Brazil in 2003 was composed of 737 MSEs and 841 medium and large firms. Perceptions regarding tax rates and tax administration as major or severe obstacles to growth do not differ statistically between the two groups, averaging 84 and 66 percent, respectively.

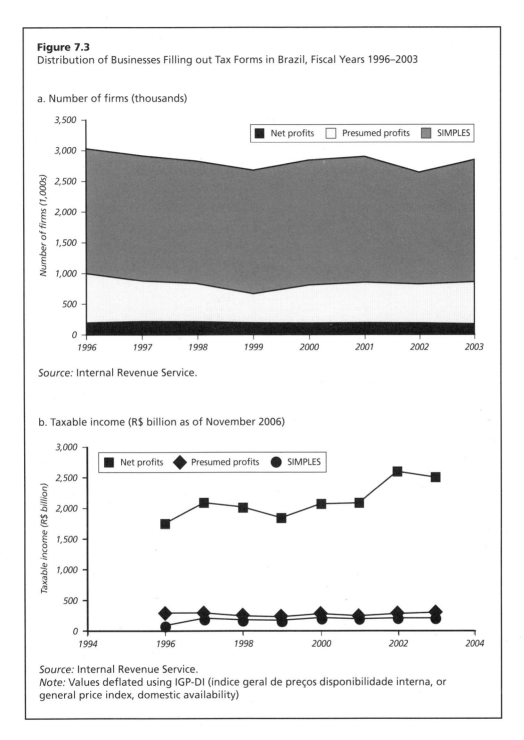

Figure 7.3
Distribution of Businesses Filling out Tax Forms in Brazil, Fiscal Years 1996–2003

a. Number of firms (thousands)

Source: Internal Revenue Service.

b. Taxable income (R$ billion as of November 2006)

Source: Internal Revenue Service.
Note: Values deflated using IGP-DI (índice geral de preços disponibilidade interna, or general price index, domestic availability)

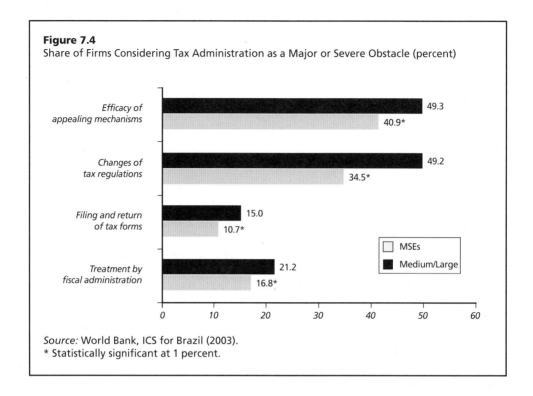

Figure 7.4
Share of Firms Considering Tax Administration as a Major or Severe Obstacle (percent)

Source: World Bank, ICS for Brazil (2003).
* Statistically significant at 1 percent.

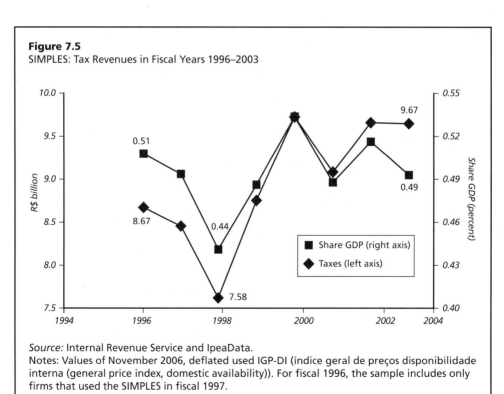

Figure 7.5
SIMPLES: Tax Revenues in Fiscal Years 1996–2003

Source: Internal Revenue Service and IpeaData.
Notes: Values of November 2006, deflated used IGP-DI (índice geral de preços disponibilidade interna (general price index, domestic availability)). For fiscal 1996, the sample includes only firms that used the SIMPLES in fiscal 1997.

Finally, the SIMPLES legislation has had a neutral impact on tax revenues.[11] Given the lower, progressive tax rates established by the SIMPLES legislation, an initial decrease in tax revenues from firms choosing to use the system was expected. This did occur in fiscal years 1997 and 1998, totaling a decline of 12.5 percent during 1996–98. After this period, however, the trend turned positive again. In addition, as a share of GDP, SIMPLES tax revenues now follow closely the movement of tax revenues overall, with the exception of fiscal year 2003 (see figure 7.5).[12]

Sustaining and Broadening the Reform

The evidence from the SIMPLES reform so far is very positive, being reflected in increases in formalization of employment, increases in investments made by enterprises, and simplification of business procedures, with no apparent loss of tax revenues. However, extending this system is a challenge. It is important to understand that the SIMPLES system involved three simultaneous actions: (a) a simplification of procedures, through the adoption of a flat tax rate, (b) a shift in the base of some taxes (the most important one being the shift of taxes from the payroll bill to gross revenues), and (c) a decrease in the average tax rate for eligible firms.

It is obviously difficult to disentangle the relative contribution of each of these three factors to the positive impacts of the regime. Nevertheless, generalizing the SIMPLES for more firms in the economy is a challenge in each of these dimensions. The adoption of a flat tax rate on gross revenues is a positive move for MSEs, but its cascading effects do not recommend its extension to medium and large firms, given the negative impact on exports and the pro-import bias associated with this kind of tax. The shift in the tax base is limited by the already high level of taxation, which requires high rates for almost all taxes imposed in the country.[13] Finally, tax revenues are needed to balance the public budget in Brazil, leading to permanent concern over the possibility of revenue losses and thus limiting the generalization of a lower tax rate.

Nonetheless, the success of SIMPLES has encouraged the government to search for opportunities to extend the reform further. Consequently, on December 14, 2006, the legislature enacted Complementary Law no. 123/2006, called the General Law for Micro and Small Enterprises. The approval of this

---

11. Tax revenues declined 12.5 percent during fiscal 1996 to fiscal 1998.

12. The correlation between SIMPLES tax revenues and SIMPLES tax revenues as a share of GDP was 82.2 percent during fiscal 1996–2003.

13. For instance, exercises show that if a single value added tax were introduced to replace the several existent value added taxes in the country, the tax rate would have to be above 30 percent, a rate much higher than the one observed in other countries: in Latin America the average value added tax hovers around 21 percent.

legislation had been delayed precisely because of its projected impact on tax revenues, a difficult option in a scenario of increasing budget expenditures and tight fiscal policy. One of its sections details the tax regime under which MSEs will operate starting in July 2007. The new tax system for SMEs is called Super SIMPLES or National SIMPLES. Its main feature is the unification of six federal taxes (which was done by the SIMPLES) with one state tax (ICMS) and one municipal tax (ISS). The qualifications to be considered micro or small remain the same as for the original SIMPLES legislation, but now firms in more sectors are eligible to participate in the scheme, including those operating in accounting, informatics, repair, and construction. About 2 million firms that have already adopted the SIMPLES are expected to benefit from this process, with an average tax reduction of 15–20 percent. Another 200,000 firms should adopt the National SIMPLES, getting an average tax break of 40–60 percent. This is expected to produce a decline in federal tax revenues of about R$2.7 billion in 2007 and R$5 billion in the following years. However, policy makers expect 3 million firms to become formal enterprises.

Conclusions

The SIMPLES reform is a good example of a successful intervention targeting a specific segment of the economy—MSEs—of relevance to policy makers worldwide. By introducing an optional flat tax for these firms, the new regime greatly simplified tax procedures for MSEs, leading to greater efficiency in the administration of the tax system, while introducing important incentives toward formalization of firms. So far, results seem to be very positive, with rigorous tests providing evidence of increased formalization and investments, higher levels of productivity, and no apparent loss of tax revenues. The impacts of recent legislation expanding this reform are still unknown. There are clear obstacles to extending the SIMPLES reform to larger firms, and a broad package of tax reforms, going beyond MSEs, remains a challenge for Brazil.

The Emergence of India's Software Sector

India's software sector grew rapidly over the past decade. In 2005–06 India's software and related services industry, which includes information technology-enabling services (ITES),[14] grew 28 percent, accounting for 4.8 percent of GDP compared with 0.5 percent in 1996–97 (NASSCOM 2006c). Several explanations have been put forward to account for the success of the industry, but

---

14. IT-enabling services include human resources, customer care, payment services, and finance.

sector-specific reforms seem largely responsible for the tremendous growth (ILO 1997, ch. 3; IMF 2005; Kumar and Joseph 2005; Nagala 2005). Performance-enhancing policies include creation of the Ministry of Information Technology, the establishment of software technology parks, as well as interventions with regard to foreign direct investment, taxation, external trade, and education.

India's success provides valuable lessons for investment climate reforms. It shows that, if designed properly, sector reforms allow governments to provide tailored solutions that not only can enhance the performance of one industry, but also can foster economic growth across the economy. It also shows that continuing efforts are necessary to sustain the impact of reform. Recently the Indian government has struggled to respond to the demands of the software sector for efforts to overhaul the education system and make it more responsive to its needs. NASSCOM, the National Association of Software and Services Companies, has predicted that India's information technology (IT) sector will be short half a million professionals by 2010 (Rai 2006). To continue as an IT powerhouse, India's government must rapidly reform its education and training programs.

The Context of Reform

Setting policy initiatives and institutional interventions aside, at least two key factors have supported the tremendous growth of India's software and related services industry. First, India's relative abundance of highly skilled labor facilitated the country's successful entry into the production and exportation of software, which require a high level of sophisticated skills. Since its independence, building on the legacy of the Nehruvian period, India's education policies have focused on excellence in higher education and prioritized science and engineering rather than social sciences and the arts. The advantage of having a large pool of English speakers has contributed to the rapid expansion of India's software sector and made it an important outsourcing destination.

Second, technological advances have played an important role in the development of India's software and related services sector. The information and communications technology (ICT) revolution made it possible to perform services, such as business process activities, in different locations and deliver them over long distances at reasonable cost. India has been a particular beneficiary to this trend, experiencing a rapid acceleration in software exports and business process outsourcing (BPO) activities. While these factors were crucial, they alone cannot explain the continuous high growth rate of India's software sector. According to NASSCOM (2006b), the Indian IT-ITES sector (including the domestic and exports segments) is expected to exceed $47.8 billion in annual revenues in fiscal year 2007, contributing an estimated 5.4 percent to GDP (up from 4.8 percent in fiscal year 2006).[15]

Another development taking place in the industry is the rapid increase of business process outsourcing. In 1993–94, almost 62 percent of all IT exports from India were conducted at the clients' location (that is, onsite). By 2002–03, offshoring became the dominant mode of delivery for software exports, accounting for almost 58 percent of total exports (IMF 2005). In May 2006 NASSCOM predicted that ITES-BPO exports would reach $6.3 billion by the end of the fiscal year, growing nearly 48 percent (NASSCOM 2006c).

Initiating the Reform

The Indian government fostered the emergence of BPO and the continuous expansion of the software and related services industry sector through a range of policy initiatives and institutional interventions.

Although an explicit software policy was not announced until 1986, in the early 1970s India's government implemented a range of measures aimed at strengthening the position of the domestic software sector. Most important, in 1970, the Indian government, as the "first developing country to do so," established the Department of Electronics (ILO 1997: ch. 3). Its early computer policies aimed to promote the domestic software and hardware industry. The dual objective of fostering both the domestic software and the domestic hardware industries created "policy contradictions, which placed some obstacles in front of software developers" (ILO 1997: ch. 3). The high import duties on computers and software made it especially expensive for firms to specialize in the production of software.

In the mid-1970s, Indian firms started to enter software exports. The creation of Tata Consulting Services in 1974 marked "the birth" of India's software export industry (Heeks 1996). The government modified its computer policy in 1984 and started to encourage software exports and export-oriented foreign investment. Policy makers had encouraged software exports from the onset, but it was this "Computer Policy of 1984 that gave a special thrust to software development by highlighting the need for institutional and policy support on a number of fronts" (Kumar and Joseph 2005: 100). These early interventions built the foundations for the emergence of a vibrant software sector in India.

---

15. The fiscal year for the Indian economy follows a 12-month cycle spanning April to March. Hence all figures reported for the current fiscal year (fiscal 2007) pertain to the industry performance during April–December 2006, which have been used to arrive at the year-end estimates.

Implementing the Reform

In 1986 Indian authorities announced a new software policy and identified the software industry as a key sector in India's agenda for export promotion. The new policy brought further liberalization and simplified the existing procedures and regulations. It also granted commercial incentives, such as tax holidays, a tax exemption on income from software exports, export subsidies, and the duty-free import of any hardware or software to be used exclusively for export purposes (Kumar and Joseph 2005).

The Indian government continued its reform efforts in the late 1980s when it attempted to create a legal and regulatory framework that would allow foreign IT companies to establish export-oriented, foreign-owned, and foreign-operated software development centers. Texas Instruments was one of the first companies to establish a 100 percent export-oriented subsidiary in India (ILO 1997: ch. 3). Building on this initial success, the Indian government created Software Technology Parks of India (STPI), which established technology parks in Bangalore, Pune, and Bhubaneshwar in 1990 (Kumar and Joseph 2005). STPI is an export-oriented scheme for the development and export of computer software. It provides physical infrastructure, freedom for 100 percent foreign equity investment, and tax incentives. In 2005 more than 5,800 businesses were registered under STPI's umbrella, accounting for a staggering 95 percent of software exports on the national level (STPI 2006).

Under the Rao government's liberalization program of 1991, the investment climate of India's software sector improved further. New policy measures were implemented, including the removal of barriers to the entry of foreign companies; the removal of restrictions on foreign technology transfers; the participation of the private sector in policy making; provisions to finance software development through equity and venture capital; the enhancement of data communications facilities; and the reduction and rationalization of taxes, duties, and tariffs (STPI 2006). In the course of the 1990s India's government also launched a range of telecommunications reforms, leading to a reduction in telecom costs and improved access for the masses.

Another crucial institutional intervention was to convert the Department of Electronics into the Ministry of Information Technology in 2000. "Until the Ministry of Information Technology was formed, there was no single apex institution or focal point for formulating national policies and strategies for the IT sector ... and the lack of any central oversight and a critical mass of in-house expertise in the public sector often hinder[ed] the sharing of information ... and the development of information standards and protocols and common information infrastructures" (Nagala 2005: 4). Today the ministry (now called the Ministry of Communications and Information Technology) is a focal point for the promotion of the software sector.

Education also played an important role in the development of India's software export capacities, as did India's historical abundance of skilled labor. The government, however, invested serious efforts in augmenting the supply of highly skilled manpower (ILO 1998). India's authorities expanded IT training and permitted private investment in IT education from the early 1980s onward. Today private sources bear about half of higher education expenditures, and approximately 85 percent of undergraduate engineering education is under private management (World Bank 2005a: ch. 5).

Sustaining and Broadening the Reform

Despite investment in IT education, the quality of India's IT institutions varies substantially. In recent years, IT companies and associations, such as Tata Consulting and NASSCOM, have complained frequently about the mismatch between the needs of the markets and the skills of graduates and workers.

This gap between sector needs and skills could threaten the sustained growth of India's software sector. According to a recent McKinsey study, "India's vast supply of graduates is smaller than it seems once their suitability for employment by multinational companies is considered" (Farrell, Kaka, and Stuërze 2005: 75). The study shows that multinationals, looking for talent in the emerging world, consider employing only 10–25 percent of the country's graduates. As a result, by 2010 the domestic IT sector will be short half a million professionals (Rai 2006).

Software and outsourcing companies have begun to take actions to improve the situation. Tata Consulting, Infosys, Wipro, and other players have set up training centers and provided course materials to universities and educational institutions to train students on topics most relevant to their business needs. The approach has been successful so far: Tata Consultancy has managed to reduce its training program from 76 days three years ago to 52 days (Rai 2006).

Albeit successful, private sector measures alone will not be able to close the growing skills deficit. The Indian government must rapidly reform its education system and training programs if it is to respond better to the needs of an innovation economy (World Bank 2005a: ch. 5).

The Impacts of Reform

In the past few years India has established itself as global hub for information and communications technologies. Services and software exports are the mainstay of the sector, with an estimated export growth of more than 32 percent for fiscal 2007 (NASSCOM 2007). India is the global leader in the provision

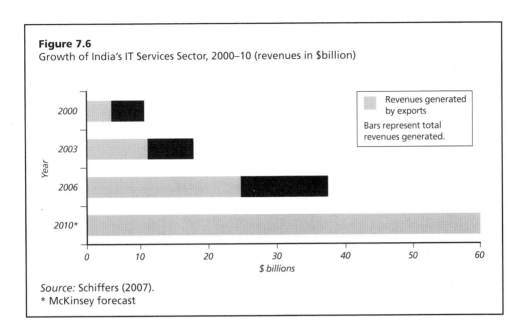

Figure 7.6
Growth of India's IT Services Sector, 2000–10 (revenues in $billion)

Source: Schiffers (2007).
* McKinsey forecast

of BPO, exporting $25 billion a year worth of these services, a figure that is expected to reach $60 billion by 2010 (Schiffers 2007; see also figure 7.6).

Key business infrastructure has improved significantly over the last decade. Due to carefully crafted government polices, the costs of international connectivity have declined rapidly, while access, penetration, and usage have improved significantly. Telecom penetration has expanded from a modest 3.6 percent in 2001 to more than 12.6 percent in 2006 and is on target to reach 19.6 percent by 2009 (NASSCOM 2007).

Enabling business policies have played a key role in the expansion of India's software sector. IT firms today "enjoy minimal regulatory and policy restrictions along with a broad range of fiscal and procedural incentives offered by the central as well as individual state governments" (see RIS 2007: 2). This has created wide-ranging employment opportunities. The total direct employment in India's IT-ITES sector has grown more than a million—from 284,000 in fiscal 1999–2000 to 1.3 million in fiscal 2005–06—and is expected to reach 1.6 million in fiscal 2007 (NASSCOM 2006a, 2006b). NASSCOM estimates that the sector has created an additional 3 million jobs through indirect and induced employment (NASSCOM 2006a).

The establishment of STPI has also supported the rapid growth of the sector and attracted new investments. More than 5,800 businesses were registered under the STPI umbrella in 2005. To continue to offer the benefits of technology parks (the existing term of the STPI scheme is ending in 2009), the government has decided to introduce similar provisions in the special economic zones.

Conclusions

The tremendous growth of India's software and related services sector is the result of a range of government measures, including policy initiatives and institutional interventions. While many of the circumstances are specific to the Indian context, countries aiming to take advantage of information and communications technologies can potentially learn from India's experiences.

An analysis of India's reform efforts shows that sector reforms can be an important catalyst for economic growth. India's government started very early on to encourage the local software sector and has supported its growth through continuous and tailored policy changes.

India's experiences also show that sector reforms (and investment climate reforms in general) require continuous oversight and efforts to sustain the impacts of reform. The expansion of India's software and related services sector has been impressive, but the government cannot afford to be complacent and rest on this success. To remain an ICT powerhouse, India has to take action and reform its education and training policies.

Building a Respected Corporate Tax System in South Africa

Over the past decade, South Africa has greatly strengthened its tax system and improved the competitiveness of its tax position globally, including in relation to Brazil and India. The new government that took over in 1994 after the end of the apartheid regime inherited a tax system rife with inefficiencies and poor compliance. Since then, the government has stabilized the country's finances, seeking to maintain a competitive tax regime and heightened fiscal discipline. Today the tax policy and administration are considered broadly appropriate to the country's economic conditions and supportive of its economic goals.

According to the investment climate survey in South Africa, only 19 percent of managers consider tax rates to be a serious constraint, compared to 84 percent in Brazil and 28 percent in India (World Bank 2007a); although 19 percent is sufficient to place tax rates among the top five concerns cited by South African managers, it is lower than in all but three of the 52 countries in which investment climate surveys had been conducted by mid-2005. Just 11 percent of managers in South Africa view tax administration as a key constraint, compared to 66 percent of their counterparts in Brazil and 27 percent in India (World Bank 2007a).

While the private sector is relatively satisfied with South Africa's tax system, more than a decade of reforms has brought clear benefits for the government as well. Despite reductions in the corporate income tax, government revenues have increased substantially. From a base of 100 in 1995, revenue derived from taxes on companies had doubled to 200.8 by 2000–01 and more than doubled again to 410.9 by 2003 (World Bank 2007a). This reflects not just improved profitability of South African firms, but also improved enforcement of tax regulations, an increase in the company register, and better compliance by registered firms.

This case study analyzes how South Africa achieved this transformation. The focus is on the reforms and reform process, recognizing that comparisons of tax rates across countries are highly complex. An examination of South Africa's experience in revising its corporate tax system can be relevant to other emerging economies, particularly Brazil, where efforts to boost public revenues in the 1990s brought rising tax rates, falling compliance, and increased informality (with the exception of the SIMPLES reform for MSEs). The lessons might also be of value to South African policy makers when considering how to approach reform related to issues other than taxation.

The Context for Reform

The formation of a new government in South Africa in 1994 constituted a turning point in South Africa's economic performance, including the development of its tax regime. Previous governments had tinkered with the tax system for decades, looking for ways to boost revenues and stimulate growth. A variety of commissions considered tax reforms, including reductions in corporate taxes. Some, such as the Margo Commission, which released its report in 1987, even prompted the government to implement many of its recommendations, and yet the need for tax reform continued to intensify (Margo Commission 1987).

The distortions created by the apartheid system limited the impact of reforms. Under apartheid, the economy was essentially cut off from the rest of the world. Investment and growth were falling, inflation and interest rates were high, and the public finances were weak (Nowak and Ricci 2005: ch. 1). Military expenditures spiraled, while the total level of taxation increased from 17 percent in 1970 to 22 percent in 1994 (Koch, Schoeman, and Van Tonder 2005: 194). More particularly, inefficiencies and distortions were endemic to the tax system. Taxpayers believed that they were overtaxed, and tax brackets continued to creep. Reforms to strengthen the public finances were crucial in fostering stronger economic progress, including key measures to improve the accountability and competitiveness of the corporate tax regime.

The new government enjoyed the benefit of making a fresh start and had more freedom to act, not least in reintegrating South Africa into the global economy. However, this is not to understate the critical economic and social challenges facing the new leadership. The majority of the population lived in poverty, facing high unemployment and poor access to key services from education to health.

Implementing Reform

Building consensus within the government on the reforms needed to improve the performance of the tax system was among the first issues to be addressed by the new South African government. To this end, the Katz Commission played a crucial role.

On June 22, 1994, the government announced the formation of a commission of inquiry with the broad mandate to review the tax structure of South Africa. Chaired by Professor Michael Katz, the Katz Commission went on to make recommendations in a series of reports from 1994 until 1999. These formed a solid basis for policy making, both for revising the institutional frameworks of the tax system and for making changes in policy.

The first report in December 1994 set some fundamental positions as a framework for policy makers (van Blerck 1995). These included several core goals:

- Corporate tax rates that are internationally competitive and domestically appropriate;
- An efficient tax administration that prevents distortion and collects taxes, in a manner that is seen to be fair and consistent, allowing for planning by the business community;
- A tax system that is friendly to foreign investors, while not discriminating against domestic business.

The Katz Commission recommendations provided a framework of priorities for reforming the tax administration and created momentum for change among decision makers, offering benefits to both the government (seeking to broaden the tax base and revenues) and business (wanting clearer procedures and more competitive rates). A remarkable number of its recommendations were implemented. While the reform efforts of previous administrations struggled to produce results, the new government focused on core goals: they recognized that the series of past reforms had left a host of complex procedures in need of simplification, and they targeted the delivery of a broader tax base at a lower rate to increase revenue (Van Rensburg 1990).

The Katz Commission's initial report in December 1994 made a strong case for avoiding any rise in corporate taxes and making tax rates more competitive. By that stage the new government had already cut the corporate income tax to 35 percent, building on a substantial cut from 48 to 40 percent in 1993 at the end of the previous administration. With the exception of an immediate increase in 1994 in the secondary tax on distributed products, which was reversed two years later, the government established a policy that continues to this day of seeking to maintain an attractive low standard rate of corporate tax and holding rates steady until higher revenues have created room for further cuts.[16] The corporate income tax was cut again to 30 percent in 1999. These changes left an effective company tax rate of 37.78 percent in 1999 if all profits were distributed, compared to a combined rate of 48 percent in 1996 (Cronje 2002; Manuel 2002).

In addition to a competitive policy on corporate tax rates, the government soon recognized the need to reform the tax administration. On October 18, 1995, the cabinet approved the creation of an independent revenue authority: the South African Revenue Service (SARS). This shifted responsibilities for tax administration from the Inland Revenue Directorate and the Customs and Excise Directorate to the new agency, which was up and running by 1997.[17] The reform met the Katz Commission's recommendation to establish an independent authority with control of its own budget, policies, and personnel. Policy makers agreed that a new authority was necessary to improve administration and collection, taking on the issues of large-scale tax evasion and ineffective countering of avoidance, and to reduce the considerable tax gap, estimated to be around R21 billion (Manuel 2002; Steenekamp 1996).

SARS quickly set about improving the tax system, implementing measures to boost efficiency of tax collection, addressing tax immorality, improving the quality and commitment of staff, and improving the capacity to audit, investigate, and prosecute tax offenders (Manuel 2002). Reforms continued into the new millennium, when the government, satisfied with changes to date, sought to improve the administrative capacity of SARS and launched further initiatives, including imposition of a capital gains tax in 2001.[18] Looking to be competitive with capital gains regimes in OECD countries and fellow emerging economies such as Brazil and Chile, the capital gains tax was set at 15 percent, with relief allowed for corporate reorganizations. Special allowances for strategic industrial projects were introduced in 2001, to be followed by a more favorable regime for depreciating the manufacturing assets of firms (Manuel 2005).

The Impacts of Reform

South Africa's experience with tax reform over the past decade has greatly contributed to the country's overall fiscal stabilization. The new government made

---

16. In 1994 the government increased the secondary tax on corporations (STC) to 25 percent. However, this increase was soon reversed, as the STC rate was halved to 12.5 percent in 1996 (Steenekamp 1996: 3).

17. The South African Revenue Service Act 34 of 1997 gave the service the mandate to collect all revenues that are due, ensure maximum compliance with the legislation, and provide a customs service that will maximize revenue collection, protect the borders, and facilitate trade. Responsibility for setting tax policy remained with the National Treasury.

18. The government also introduced the residence principle of taxation at this time, further increasing conformity with international tax norms.

major strides in raising growth and living standards. Real GDP grew at nearly 3 percent on average from 1995 to 2003 and double that from 1980 to 1994 (Nowak and Ricci 2005: p. 2).

The Katz Commission helped to provide the government with immediate reforms that could be "quick wins," building momentum beginning with the 1995 budget and then helping to shape medium- and long-term reform.

Government policy and a new tax administration improved fairness in the system and established a global presence for South African companies. The reforms led to a broadening of the tax base and higher levels of compliance: government revenue targets have been consistently exceeded. This provided fiscal space for further reductions in company income tax rates. At the same time, the overall improvement in fiscal performance contributed to lower real interest rates. Combined with productivity gains, the lower interest rates helped to counteract higher business costs (Nowak and Ricci 2005: 3).

Over the past decade, the government has been able to reduce corporate tax rates steadily without allowing them to fluctuate widely. This predictability has helped investors to plan and reinforced the attractiveness of South Africa's investment climate.

In addition to policy changes, institutional improvements were also crucial. The administration of the tax system has improved significantly since the creation of SARS. The formation of the new institution marked a new beginning for the tax authorities. A higher, more independent profile and the hiring of professionally qualified staff led to improvements in performance, with benefits for firms that received a higher quality of service. The private sector could see improved transparency in the tax processes and now had a service that could be held accountable when things went wrong. The improved service boosted SARS's standing within government, with business, and with the public at-large.

SARS began to apply the law more effectively, conducting audits, and this helped to improve compliance. In 2000–01 the tax paid by companies increased 50 percent (Cronje 2002). In 1999 company taxes, excluding the secondary tax on distributed products and mining companies, contributed around 10 percent of total tax revenue for the country, but this increased to 16.8 percent by fiscal 2001–02 (Manuel 2002). Today, South Africa has been able to meet its 25 percent ratio of revenue to GDP guideline with ease, reflecting the vastly improved ability to generate revenue.[19] In the 2006–07 tax year South Africa obtained its first fiscal surplus: 0.3 percent, about R5 billion (Russell 2007: 5).

South Africa is at the forefront of competitive tax strategies in the South African Development Community (SADC) region, suggesting that the lessons of its tax reforms might be of real value, not just to middle-income competitors but

---

19. This 25 percent tax to GDP ratio is the highest in Sub-Saharan Africa and comparable with that of other emerging economies (World Bank 2006c).

to neighboring countries as well (Robinson 2005). Changes such as the introduction of a capital gains tax helped to bring South Africa's tax system further in line with international systems. The marginal effective tax rate on capital for South Africa is relatively low compared to that for OECD competitors such as Canada and Australia and remains lower than that for India and Brazil.

Sustaining and Broadening Reform

One of the strengths of the corporate tax system in South Africa has been the sustained effort to look for further improvements. The government has not been afraid to continue with reforms almost annually, not as major shifts that would create uneasiness among the business and investor communities, but as tweaks to the program following the restructuring and significant policy changes in the second half of the 1990s and 2000–01. The stability and stronger tax base that the larger reforms have helped to create have allowed for subsequent initiatives to alleviate the corporate tax burden. This can be seen in the reduction of the corporate tax rate from 30 to 29 percent in 1999, when the government was able to absorb the projected revenue loss of R2 billion (Manuel 2002; see table 7.3).

SARS has continued to streamline the efficiency and quality of its services and the administration of the tax system. Having improved the quality and responsiveness of its own staff, in 2004 it introduced legislation to improve the regulation of tax consultants and advisers and promote better compliance (Manuel 2005). The improvements in service and outreach to large corporations have generated a strong culture of tax compliance. However, improving service remains an ongoing challenge, with no room for complacency.

One area that has become a focus for reform is improving the participation of small businesses in the tax system and making the tax burden on smaller firms

Table 7.3
Corporate Tax Burden in South Africa, 1995 and 2006

Tax rate	1995	2006
Corporate tax	35	29
Small business with turnover rate less than R35,000	—	0
Small business with turnover between R35,000 and R250,000	—	10
Secondary tax on corporations (STC)	25	12.5
Maximum effective rate of corporate tax and STC	48	37.8

Source: 1995 data comes from Manuel (2002). 2006 data from "South Africa: Summary of the Domestic Taxation Regime," http://lowtax.net/lowtax/html/offon/southafrica/sasummary.html.
Note: The maximum effective rate applies to companies that distribute all of their after-tax profits as dividends.
— Not available.

more manageable. In its first years of operation, SARS did little in practice to encourage the participation of small businesses, focusing on increasing compliance among large and medium-size firms. Recognizing this issue, the government began to promote small business development with tax concessions introduced in the first years of the millennium.[20]

However, even with reforms made in the past five years, small businesses face disproportionate costs in terms of time and money, and they have relatively little influence on tax policy. The Small Business Project has found that managing and paying "company and operating taxes" are significant administrative barriers for small firms (Small Business Project 2004). Current policy development continues to give priority to empowering small business, reducing rates, giving relief for filing obligations, and having SARS put together a package of interventions to assist small businesses, not just with their tax issues but with broader business management, offering support services, such as tax helpers, help desks, accounting packages, and extended hours, free of charge (Manuel 2005). Changes to corporate taxes in 2006 were minor but did include further changes to attract the participation of small businesses.[21]

Another area where reform continues to be sustained is the simplification of tax procedures. The first Katz Commission interim report in 1994 found that the secondary tax on corporations (STC) was essentially making foreign corporations pay the maximum rate of corporate tax and distorting the financing decisions of firms. The commission recommended looking for alternatives to the STC in the form of an imputation tax, yet this issue remains unresolved.[22] While the corporate income tax rate is very competitive internationally, the imposition of the STC raises the effective corporate tax rate significantly. Today the STC remains at a rate of 12.5 percent on distributions, although dividends paid within a group of companies are exempt. Foreign companies operating through a branch or agency in South Africa currently face a tax rate of 34 percent (reduced in the past year from 35 percent). However, in the 2007 budget speech, Trevor Manuel, finance minister, pleased business with the announcement that

---

20. The government introduced a graduated corporate tax rate of 15 percent on the first R150,000 of taxable income for qualifying small firms with a gross income of R3 million or less in 2000 (the threshold was raised to R5 million in 2003), a 100 percent accelerated depreciation deduction for plant and machinery used by small firms for manufacturing and similar processes and a double deduction for the first R20,000 of start-up costs of a new business in 2003 (Manuel 2002). See also "South Africa: Summary of the Domestic Taxation Regime," http: //lowtax.net/ lowtax/html/offon/southafrica/sasummary.html.

21. Proposed changes in the 2006 budget included adjusting tax brackets for qualifying small businesses with turnover less than R14 million (up from R6 million) and a tax amnesty for small firms waiving taxes due up to March 31, 2004, barring a simple 10 percent nondisclosure penalty payable in 2005. See "South Africa: Summary of the Domestic Taxation Regime," http:// lowtax.net/lowtax/html/offon/southafrica/sasummary.html.

22. Of central government revenues in 2005–05, the STC represented 2 percent compared to 20 percent for corporate income tax. See Steenekamp (1996); South Africa Revenue Service, http:// www.sars.gov.za.

the STC will be reduced to 10 percent in October 2007 and then scrapped in favor of a tax on dividends to be paid by shareholders beginning at the end of 2008 (Russell 2007: 5).

While the STC is to be removed, it is not the only complicating component of the corporate tax regime in South Africa. Special conditions are applied to gold and uranium mining companies and long-term insurance companies, while social security contributions of employers are now supplemented with a "skills development levy" of 1 percent of payroll for all employers with a payroll over R500,000.[23]

Although no one sector faces an excessive tax burden, there is potential to consider the implications of the tax system for different sectors of the economy and what targeted reforms might do to reduce the tax burden, if appropriate, increase efficiencies, and stimulate sector growth. Continued reforms are crucial, as tax rates in South Africa and the SADC region as a whole remain vulnerable to global influence, particularly as economies are liberalized further.

Conclusions

The South African experience highlights the importance of simplicity and transparency in tax administration and a responsive tax administrator that can be held accountable when issues arise.

The case highlights the benefits of a stable corporate tax rate regime. By avoiding the temptation to make too large cuts or the need to increase rates, South Africa has fostered good business practices and investment by providing a predictable tax environment for business.

Above all, continued reform is crucial for the tax regime to remain competitive. The South African experience demonstrates the value of continuing to reduce rates when there is fiscal space to do so and continuing to improve tax administration procedures. The government cannot afford to rest on its laurels. In South Africa's case, policy makers are still exploring ways to bring smaller firms into the tax net.

South Africa's Accelerated and Shared Growth Initiative

Identifying priorities for reform can be one of the biggest challenges in attempts to reform the investment climate. South Africa's authorities have attempted to identify and implement reform priorities through the so-called Accelerated and Shared Growth Initiative for South Africa (ASGISA), which aims to raise

---

23. South Africa Revenue Service, http://www.sars.gov.za.

economic growth to 6 percent between 2010 and 2014 and to halve the rates of unemployment and poverty by 2014. To achieve these ambitious targets, authorities have identified what they determine to be the most binding constraints on economic growth and designed policy measures to address them. Although it is too early to evaluate the ultimate success of this approach, ASGISA can provide a useful framework for designing and assessing growth-enhancing policies (IMF 2006).

The Context of Reform

South Africa's economic performance has improved remarkably since apartheid ended in 1994. Sound macroeconomic management and structural reforms have led to faster economic growth, lower and more predictable inflation, stronger public finances, a sound financial system, and an improved external position (Lizondo and others 2006). Annual GDP growth averaged about 3.4 percent between 1995 and 2004 and reached almost 5 percent in 2005. Despite these successes, South Africa remains a highly unequal society with enormous social and economic challenges: 13 percent of the population lives in "first world" conditions, while at the other extreme, about 22 million people live in developing-country conditions.[24] According to the narrow definition of unemployment, almost 27 percent of South Africans are unemployed (37 percent according to the broader definition, which includes discouraged workers). The country also has one of the highest HIV/AIDS prevalence rates in the world, with approximately 17–21 percent of the adult population infected with HIV.

Initiating Reform

In recognition of these challenges, South Africa's authorities, led by Deputy President Phumzile Mlambo-Ncguka, launched ASGISA in 2006 with the aim of broadening and accelerating the benefits of economic growth. Key elements include acceleration of public investment in infrastructure; targeted sector interventions and reforms; improvement of education and skills development programs; and stronger public service delivery. From a policy-making perspective, however, specific processes surrounding the formulation of ASGISA can be as informative as key elements of the initiative itself. Specifically, ASGISA shows how using analytical frameworks and diagnostic tools can contribute to the process of identifying priorities for reform and building support among key stakeholders.

---

24. See http://web.worldbank.org/WBSITE/EXTERNAL/COUNTRIES/AFRICAEXT/SOUTHAFR ICAEXTN/0,,menuPK:368086~pagePK:141132~piPK:141107~theSitePK:368057,00.html.

Identifying Priorities for Reform

The South African government formed a task force to carry out the analytical work needed to identify the priorities for the reform process.[25] The deputy president's task force included the Ministry of Finance, Ministry of Trade and Industry, Ministry of Public Enterprises, and regional authorities, as well as domestic and international experts.[26] The task force analyzed the capabilities and deficiencies of South Africa's economy using the "binding constraints approach." Recently developed by leading international economists, this approach allowed the task force to identify key constraints on economic growth and develop policies to address them (see box 7.2). The International Monetary Fund (IMF 2006: 27) states in its recent staff report about South Africa, "ASGISA should provide a useful framework for designing and assessing growth-enhancing policies ... The ASGISA growth targets appear reachable. ... Many of the constraints on growth identified under ASGISA are ... widely recognized to be critical for South Africa's growth potential." To help in decision making, the task force drew on diagnostic tools, such as the World Bank investment climate surveys and Doing Business data.

The investment climate surveys, in which respondents identify their leading business constraints, offer valuable insights into what hinders enhanced economic growth in South Africa (see World Bank 2007a). Worker skills, macroeconomic instability, labor regulations, and crime are rated as the biggest constraints. Between 29 and 35 percent of enterprises rate each of these areas as a major problem, compared to less than 20 percent for all other areas (see figure 7.7).

The managers surveyed identify worker skills as the key obstacle to their enterprises' operations and growth. Firms have to pay a high premium to attract skilled and educated workers. Despite these concerns, relatively few enterprises have training programs. According to investment climate surveys, between 70 and 80 percent of skilled workers in China, Brazil, and Poland receive training compared to fewer than half of skilled workers in South Africa.

Despite positive economic growth and moderate inflation, macroeconomic instability is the second greatest constraint raised in the investment climate surveys. About 33 percent of South African firms rate macroeconomic instability as a serious concern, and this negative perception seems to derive from the instability of the South African exchange rate. Between 2000 and 2002, the rand depreciated against major currencies, falling about 27 percent against the U.S. dollar, in real terms. After appreciating rapidly over the next four years, espe-

---

25. The government has consulted a range of stakeholders, including a panel of international academic experts who will provide further advice over the next two years. For more details, see http://www.info.gov.za/asgisa/.

26. The international panel consists of economists and international experts from Harvard University, Massachusetts Institute of Technology, University of Michigan, and other institutions.

Box 7.2   Accelerated and Shared Growth Initiative for South Africa

Although ASGISA is still a work in progress, it has identified six key constraints to growth and is formulating proposals to address some of them (based on IMF 2006: 22):

1. *The level and volatility of the exchange rate.* The volatility of the rand is thought to be deterring investment in tradable goods and services that are not commodity based. The rand has also been perceived as overvalued in the sense that economic resources have been diverted into narrow areas of investment.
2. *Inadequate infrastructure and logistics.* The government plans to invest the equivalent of about 20 percent of 2005 GDP over the next three years on transport, communications, and power provision by public enterprises; housing and social institutions; and provincial projects (in agriculture, mining, and other areas).
3. *Shortage of skills.* Measures in this area include the Joint Initiative for Priority Skills Acquisition, a new committee with representatives from government, business, labor, and education, charged with identifying and addressing urgent skills shortages. The immediate focus will be on the skills needed for infrastructure development, public service delivery, and sectors identified under ASGISA as priorities (for example, tourism).
4. *Barriers to entry and competition.* Competition policy is being reviewed to find ways to reduce input costs and promote "downstream" sectors like metal fabrication, machinery, and plastics. Discriminatory pricing practices that favor exports over domestic markets (so-called import parity pricing) have been targeted. Duties on certain steel products, for example, have been removed to facilitate greater import competition.
5. *The regulatory environment.* A current review includes plans to introduce one-stop shops for starting businesses, a system for analyzing regulatory impact, and improved planning at provincial and local levels. The environmental impact assessment system will also be reformed.
6. *Limited capacity within government.* Project Consolidate aims to improve provincial and local administration, including through the deployment of skilled professionals where they are needed most.

Development finance institutions will be reviewed, and other initiatives are being considered under the ASGISA framework:

- *Sectoral investment and industrial strategies.* A number of sectors have been earmarked for special support, starting with outsourcing and tourism (together expected to create half a million jobs). Investment in research and development will also be supported.
- *Second economy interventions.* These include support for SMEs and black economic empowerment through, for example, preferential procurement; improved access to small-scale credit; and the provision of employment through the Expanded Public Works Program. The impact of labor laws on SMEs is also being reviewed.

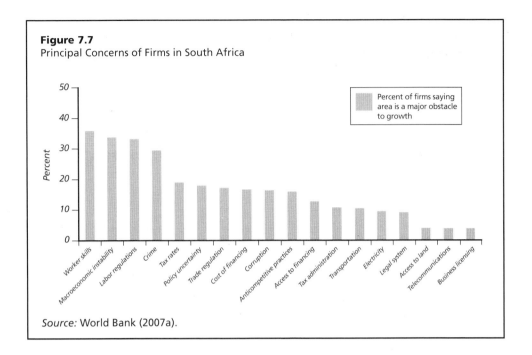

Figure 7.7
Principal Concerns of Firms in South Africa

Source: World Bank (2007a).

cially against the dollar, the rand showed no clear trend in 2005 and has depreciated sharply in recent months.

Engaging Key Stakeholders

From the early stages, the South African government has emphasized that AS-GISA is a national shared-growth initiative rather than a government program. During the formulation process, the task force consulted with organized business, labor and religious leaders, as well as youth and women in various groupings and forums. In recent months, the South African policy leaders have started to disseminate the findings of the task force through the print and television media. They use high-profile events, such as President Mbeki's 2006 state of the nation address, to explain the potential benefits of the reform initiative and to mobilize grassroots support.

Conclusions

ASGISA's success and potential contribution to growth will become more evident over the next few years after its policies have been fully implemented. This analysis suggests, however, that South Africa's experience already offers at least one important lesson for countries undertaking similar reforms: using sound analytical frameworks and detailed diagnostics can help to identify reform priorities and to build support for more reform.

8
Conclusions

Brazil, India, and South Africa are increasingly important countries in the world economy. All three have a growing share of global GDP and are producing companies that are competing prominently on the international stage (see table 8.1).

However, the business environment at the national level remains crucial to continued growth, not just of leading firms but of micro, small, and medium enterprises that form the vast majority of the private sector and offer the greatest opportunities for individuals to escape poverty. A comparison of the investment climate—the platform for sustained success—of these three emerging economies suggests a number of conclusions.

The investment climates in Brazil, India, and South Africa show substantial scope for improvement. Brazil and India's positions in the Doing Business rankings are out of step with their global status at 121st and 134th, respectively, in the 2007 tables. These findings suggest that much more can be done to reduce

Table 8.1
Projected GDP in Brazil, India, and South Africa, 2000–50 (2003 US$ billion)

Year	Brazil	India	South Africa
2000	762	469	83
2010	668	929	147
2020	1,333	2,104	267
2030	2,189	4,935	447
2040	3,740	12,367	737
2050	6,074	27,803	1,174

Source: Goldman Sachs BRICs model projections. See Wilson and Purushothaman (2003).

red tape and facilitate business development. Even South Africa, with a ranking of 29th, cannot afford complacency, as the Doing Business rankings suggest that the country's business environment is not as attractive as that of a number of other emerging economies, including Chile, Malaysia, and Thailand.

There are substantial differences in the investment climate of the three countries, particularly in the facets that serve as the most binding constraints on enterprise. For example, Indian managers list electricity supply among their leading constraints, which is not considered among the leading priorities by managers in Brazil and South Africa. Similarly the availability and cost of skilled labor is the primary constraint in South Africa, but does not figure among the major constraints in Brazil or India.

However, while some of the top constraints identified by managers are striking in their differences, there are also *areas of common concern* across Brazilian, Indian, and South African business communities. Tax rates feature among the leading constraints for all three countries. In many cases, two of the countries shared a common concern at the time of survey, such as macroeconomic instability cited among top constraints in both Brazil and South Africa. Such commonalities suggest that there are policy areas of shared interest and that *Brazil, India, and South Africa can learn from the reform experiences of one another.* There remains much scope for policy makers in each country to learn from their counterparts in other emerging markets, in terms of both process and policy. For example, Brazil's successful reform of bankruptcy procedures can be instructive for India and South Africa, while India's experience with stabilizing the exchange rate can offer lessons for Brazil and South Africa (World Bank 2007b suggests that macroeconomic instability is the second most important constraint facing business in Brazil and South Africa, but not a significant issue for Indian firms).

An analysis of India's reform efforts shows that sector reforms can be an important catalyst for economic growth. India's government started very early on to encourage the local software sector and supported its growth through continuous and tailored policy changes. The tremendous growth of India's software and related services sector reflects a range of government measures, including policy initiatives and institutional interventions. While many of the circumstances are specific to the Indian context, countries aiming to take advantage of information and communications technologies could learn from India's experiences.

The South African experience highlights the importance of simple and transparent tax administration and a responsive tax administrator that can be held accountable when issues arise. The case highlights the benefits of having a stable corporate tax rate regime. By avoiding excessively large tax cuts or the need to increase rates, South Africa has fostered good business practices and investment by providing a predictable tax environment for business. This experience could be useful to both Brazil and India, where high tax rates and burdensome tax administration are major constraints on the business community.

There are significant differences within each country in the quality of the investment climate.[1] Given the size of Brazil, India, and South Africa, it is not surprising that policies at the state level have a significant impact on the local investment climate and can vary substantially, with some states regulating with a much heavier hand than others. Therefore, while it is important for countries to benchmark themselves against regional and global competitors and to set targets accordingly, it is important for them to look inward and to encourage state and municipal authorities to adopt reforms that have worked particularly well in specific parts of the country. There is fierce competition between cities to attract investors through the best regulatory environment, as seen in Brazil and India, so it is important to create incentives to monitor the impact of initiatives at the city and state level and to copy successful reforms.

There are also differences not just between states or cities, but between sectors or sizes of firm, providing additional areas where policy makers can learn from successes and failures in targeted policies. The SIMPLES reform in Brazil is a good example of a successful intervention targeting a specific segment of the economy—micro and small enterprises—that could provide lessons for others. By introducing an optional flat tax for these firms, the new regime greatly simplified the tax procedures facing small businesses, leading to greater efficiency in the administration of the tax system, while introducing important incentives toward the formalization of firms.

Investment climate reform needs to be a continuous process if the country is to remain competitive. The experiences of Brazil, India, and South Africa suggest that, to maintain a strong investment climate, there is no room for complacency. Even successful reforms require regular review and adjustments where necessary. The example of corporate tax reform in South Africa illustrates the value of continued reform to maintain the international competitiveness of the tax regime. The South African government reduced rates when it had the fiscal space to do so and continues to make regular adjustments to streamline tax administrative procedures. The impressive growth of India's software and related information technology services sector prompts envy worldwide, but this success has its roots in long-term policy decisions and continued reform efforts. India's ability to remain an information and communications technology powerhouse will depend in large part on continued reform, particularly in the area of education and training policies to ensure a large pool of skilled labor.[2]

Diagnostic tools, such as the Doing Business indicators, simulator, and results of the investment climate surveys, can help policy makers in setting reform priorities. The availability of data, both hard data and the surveys of percep-

---

1. In Brazil, opening a business in the state of Minas Gerais takes only 19 days, compared to 152 days in São Paulo. By way of comparison, the difference between the best- and worst-performing state in Mexico is only twofold. The performance of Minas Gerais places it in the top 30 worldwide in terms of the time to start a business. São Paulo ranks 149th out of 155.

2. Salaries are spiraling fast for the ICT and financial services sectors in India, and the ICT lobby group estimates a shortfall of 500,00 professionals by 2010, threatening the future of the sector in the country (Tucker 2007: 9).

tions, is crucial for informed decision making. The Doing Business indicators, enterprise survey results, and the growing arsenal of available diagnostic tools can assist policy makers to gauge potential priorities for reform in the context of both international and state- and city-level comparisons. Equally important, sound analytical frameworks and detailed diagnostics can help to build momentum for reform, demonstrating the need to foster change and challenge vested interests. While the contribution to growth of South Africa's ASGISA will only become evident over time, it reflects a new approach that recognizes the value that diagnostic tools can offer. Amid heightened global competition, emerging economies, such as Brazil, India, and South Africa, even those experiencing rapid economic growth cannot afford to ignore investment climate constraints and benefit from closely monitoring reform efforts at home and abroad in the constant search for improvement.

Appendix A
Concept of the Investment Climate

The investment climate in a country is the collective set of incentives that establish the "rules of the game" to which economic actors must adhere. Set by a wide variety of sources, including government policies, cultures of public administration, and institutional, social, and physical infrastructure, the investment climate determines the level and uncertainty of returns expected by economic agents and consequently affects the quality and quantity of investment and the incentives to employ inputs productively. The investment climate can be divided into three main areas:

- *Macroeconomic and trade policy.* The capacity of domestic institutions and economic policy (for example, fiscal, monetary, trade, and exchange rate policy, administration of customs and ports, security of property rights, strength of rule of law, and political stability) to reduce costs of international trade and finance and ensure a consistent and nondistortionary basis for investment, production, and exchange;
- *Microeconomic framework.* The contribution of microeconomic regulation (for example, rules governing market entry and exit and factor markets) and enforcement agencies to efficient, expeditious, and predictable processes of production and exchange;
- *Enabling infrastructure.* The cost, availability, and reliability of key public factors of production and exchange (for example, credit, electricity, land, knowledge, physical security, skilled employees, and transport).

None of these factors, or their components, exists in isolation, however. Indeed, there is a high degree of complementarity across domains of macroeconmic policy, regulation, and provision of public goods. The dynamics of the investment climate can be complicated. A change in policy in one facet, for instance, may lead firms to heighten their productivity, releasing binding constraints on growth by seemingly unrelated policies. When drawing implications for reform from investment climate analysis, it is important for policy makers to be aware of these interrelationships and the potential for indirect, even unintended, effects. A given set of reforms may, for instance, deliver quite different results depending on the sequence by which those reforms are implemented. Where political constraints restrict the scope of reform, as is often the case, identifying the most effective sequence of policy changes is often critical to sustaining the political case for reform.

Information on the state of a country's investment climate is provided by two separate but complementary instruments published by the World Bank: the investment climate assessment and the Doing Business report. While both publications provide invaluable information on the state of the investment climate across the world, each adopts a different approach and provides a distinct assessment of the ease of investment, production, and exchange in an economy:

- Investment climate assessments are based primarily on firm-level surveys of managerial perceptions concerning the impact of the regulation, institutions, and infrastructure. Surveys cover a stratified random sample of manufacturing firms spread across the country, and a core set of survey questions, asked of firms in every country, ensures that reports are at least partially comparable across countries;
- The Doing Business report seeks to analyze existing laws and regulations objectively through a common methodology and to consider their effect on a hypothetical firm. Much effort is expended by the Doing Business team to ensure cross-country comparability of results, and a ranking of 175 countries according to the ease of doing business is published annually.

The investment climate assessments and the Doing Business reports complement each other in a number of ways. Doing Business enables a transparent and simple comparison of the administrative and financial burdens of complying with regulation across a wide span of countries. Yet the analysis, done by legal experts in surveyed countries, relies very much on de jure regulation and may not provide an accurate assessment of effective constraints on productivity and investment where enforcement is lax or where firms operate through informal channels.[1] The Doing Business analysis also focuses on a hypothetical firm, de-

---

1. One salient example relates to the total taxation burden in the city of Rio de Janeiro. The Doing Business analysis finds that medium-size firms in Rio are required to pay a total of 201 percent of their gross profits in tax, the highest of any city in the world. Obviously, given the wide range of businesses operating in Rio, this cannot be an accurate description of the de facto tax burden.

fined in a very specific manner and located only in the country's main business center. As such, the ascribed administrative burdens and costs may not be applicable to firms with different characteristics.

Investment climate assessments directly survey managers as to their perceptions of the effective constraints on firm-level expansion and on the administrative and financial burdens of complying with government regulation.[2] Accordingly, they can provide a more realistic assessment of the effective constraints on firm-level growth. However, cross-sectional comparisons of survey results are fraught with difficulty and ordinarily provide little basis for assessing the magnitude of problems.[3] Another concern is whether survey responses accurately reflect reality, as respondents may adjust their responses in view of certain outcomes, particularly if they believe their responses can have an impact on policy.[4] Furthermore, managers of extant firms in the formal sector represent a biased sample, insofar as they have already "succeeded" in establishing their business and are unlikely to be able to provide an adequate diagnosis of the problems faced by those whom the investment climate has condemned to entrepreneurial failure.

Notwithstanding such cautions, the data obtained by the investment climate assessments and Doing Business reports collectively represent the most insightful evidence available on the impediments to investment and productivity in developing countries. Provided that the objective cardinal measures of the Doing Business database are used in a complementary fashion with the perception-based indicators of the investment climate assessments, useful summary comparisons can ordinarily be drawn across countries, and conclusions and policy recommendations can be made accordingly.

---

2. At the time of writing, the World Bank had conducted investment climate surveys across 76 countries since 2001.

3. Respondents in prosperous Indian states such as Karnataka tend to view their state's investment climate in a much more critical light than their counterparts in poorer states such as Bihar, a difference that likely reflects the differing expectations of managers in the two regions.

4. As an example, managers may overstate the amount of time spent dealing with regulation in an effort to encourage the government to reduce the regulatory burden on businesses.

Appendix B
Data Sources

This work draws on various primary and secondary resources compiled by the World Bank and the International Finance Corporation. Data for the analysis are drawn from two sources: investment climate surveys and the Doing Business database. The work also draws significantly from investment climate assessments completed by the World Bank, which analyze results of the investment climate surveys and identify key constraints on doing business imposed by the investment climate.

Investment climate surveys are employed by the World Bank Group to build a picture of a country's investment climate from the perspective of local managers. Typically, surveys generate indicators on issues such as the quality of physical infrastructure, the efficiency of factor and product markets, the prevalence of law and order, and the burden of tax and regulatory compliance. Investment climate surveys, which are normally undertaken under the auspices of a national stakeholder, such as an employers association, an indigenous development agency, or a central statistical bureau, survey managers' perceptions regarding the effective constraints on firm-level expansion and on the administrative and financial burdens of complying with government regulation.

Although investment climate surveys are individually modified to ensure that each country's survey reflects local priorities for policy reform and economic research, surveys share commonalities in the method of administering the questionnaire and selecting enterprises for inclusion in the sample. In addition, survey instruments employed by investment climate surveys share a common set of "core" questions that are administered using a common methodology in each country. These common questions constitute a well-tested product of past World Bank surveys and collectively constitute 50–60 percent of the full survey instrument, the balance being items generating information for analyzing more specialized policy issues.[1]

For Brazil, the investment climate survey was conducted between July and October 2003 and covered 1,642 manufacturing firms across 13 Brazilian states. The investment climate survey for India was conducted between March and July 2003 and covered 1,860 manufacturing firms sampled from 40 cities in 12 major states. The investment climate survey for South Africa was conducted between January and December 2004 and covered 800 firms, of which 75 percent were in the manufacturing sector, 14 percent in the construction industry, and 11 percent in the wholesale and retail trade. The references contain links to the online databases for the investment climate surveys of these three countries and others.

Investment climate assessments analyze data collected by investment climate surveys to provide a quantitative assessment of the microeconomic impact of various business constraints as identified by local managers and to enable a comparison of the country's investment climate with regional and international benchmarks. The investment climate assessment for Brazil, which spans two volumes, was published in December 2005 (World Bank 2005b). The investment climate assessment for India was published in November 2004 (World Bank 2004), although there is also reference to data from the survey conducted in 2006, which are yet to be included in a formal assessment. The investment climate assessment for South Africa was published in draft form in 2005 and finalized in a 2007 publication (World Bank 2007a).

In addition to the investment climate surveys and assessments, the book uses data collected by the Doing Business research project. The Doing Business database provides objective measures of business regulations and their enforcement. The Doing Business indicators on the regulatory costs of business are comparable across 175 economies and can be used to analyze specific regulations that either enhance or constrain investment, productivity, and growth. Together with the Doing Business reports, they can be used to examine the microeconomic impact of domestic regulation, government policies, and public infrastructure and to allow objective comparisons of the quality of investment climates across the world.

---

1.   For more on the methodology, see http://www.enterprisesurveys.org/Methodology/.

References

Beath, Andrew. 2006. "The Investment Climate in Brazil, India, South Africa: A Contribution to the IBSA Debate." Paper prepared under the supervision of Qimiao Fan, Michael Jarvis, and Jose G. Reis for the first summit of the India, Brazil, and South Africa Dialogue Forum (IBSA), Brasilia, Brazil, September. World Bank, Washington, DC, September.

Cronje, W. B. 2002. "Tax Developments in South Africa." *Intertax* 30 (6-7): 254–57.

Djankov, Simeon, Caralee McLiesh, and Andrei Shleifer. 2007. "Private Credit in 129 Countries." *Journal of Financial Economics* 84 (2): 299–329.

Dollar, David, Mary Hallward-Driemeier, and Taye Mengistae. 2004. *Investment Climate and International Integration*. Washington, DC: World Bank.

———. 2005. *Investment Climate and Firm Performance in Developing Economies*. Washington, DC: World Bank.

Escribano, Alvaro, and J. Luis Guasch. 2005. "Assessing the Impact of the Investment Climate on Productivity Using Firm-Level Data: Methodology and the Cases of Guatemala, Honduras, and Nicaragua." Policy Research Working Paper 3621. World Bank, Washington, DC, June.

Fajnzylber, Pablo, William Maloney, and Gabriel Montes Rojas. 2006. "Microenterprise Dynamics in Developing Countries: How Similar Are They to Those in the Industrialized World? Evidence from Mexico." *World Bank Economic Review* 20 (3): 389–419.

Farrell, Diana, Noshir Kaka, and Sascha Stürze. 2005. "Ensuring India's Offshoring Future." *McKinsey Quarterly Special Edition: Fulfilling India's Promise.*

Fernandez, Enric, and Poonam Gupta. 2006. "Understanding the Growth Momentum in India's Services." In Catriona Purfield and Jerald Schiff, eds.,

India Goes Global: Its Expanding Role in the World Economy. Washington, DC: International Monetary Fund.

Heeks, Richard. 1996. *India's Software Industry: State Policy, Liberalization, and Industrial Development.* New Delhi: Sage Publications.

ILO (International Labour Organisation). 1997. *The Evolution of the Indian Software Industry.* Geneva: ILO.

————. 1998. *World Employment Report 1998–99: Employability in the Global Economy; How Training Matters.* Geneva: ILO.

IMF (International Monetary Fund). 2005. *India: Selected Issues.* IMF Country Report 05/87, March. Washington, DC: IMF.

————. 2006. "South Africa." Staff report prepared for the 2006 Article IV consultation. IMF Country Report 6/327. Washington, DC: IMF, September.

Koch, Steven, Niek J. Schoeman, and Jurie J. Van Tonder. 2005. "Economic Growth and the Structure of Taxes in South Africa: 1960–2002." *South Africa Journal of Economics* 73 (2, June): 190–210.

Kumar, Nagesh, and K. J. Joseph. 2005. "Export of Software and Business Process Outsourcing from Developing Countries: Lessons from the Indian Experience." *Asia-Pacific Trade and Investment Review* 1 (1, April): 91–110.

Lizondo, Saul, and others. 2006. *South Africa: Selected Issues.* IMF Country Report 6/328. Washington, DC: International Monetary Fund.

Manuel, Trevor. 2002. "The South African Tax Reform Experience since 1994." Presentation given by the minister of finance at the Annual Conference of the International Bar Association, October 24.

————. 2005. "Budget Speech 2005." Speech given by the minister of finance, February 23.

Margo Commission. 1987. *Report of the Commission of Inquiry into the Tax Structure of the Republic of South Africa* [The Margo Commission Report]. RP34/1987. Pretoria: Government Printer.

Monteiro, Joana C. M., and Juliano Assunção. 2006. "Outgoing the Shadows: Estimating the Impact of Bureaucracy Simplification and Tax Cut on Formality and Investment." Paper presented at the Universidade Federal do Rio de Janeiro, Seminários de Pesquisa, September 5.

Nagala, Sarala V. 2005. "India's Story of Success: Promoting the Information Technology Industry." *Stanford Journal of International Relations* 6 (1, Winter). (Available at http://www.stanford.edu/group/sjir/6.1.05_nagala .html.)

NASSCOM (National Association of Software and Services Companies). 2006a. "Indian IT Industry: NASSCOM Analysis." May.

————. 2006b. "Indian IT Sector Score 10-in-10." May.

————. 2006c. "Key Highlights of Indian ITES-BPO Sector Performance." May.

———. 2007. "Strategic Review 2007: Executive Summary."

Nowak, Michael, and Luca A. Ricci. 2005. *Post-Apartheid South Africa: The First Ten Years*. Washington, DC: International Monetary Fund.

Rai, Saritha. 2006. "India's Outsourcing Industry Is Facing a Labor Shortage." *New York Times*, February 16.

RIS (Research and Information System for Developing Countries). 2007. *Indian IT Industry: Lessons for Mekong Countries*. Mekong-Ganga Policy Brief 1, March. (http://www.ris.org.in/MGPB1.pdf.)

Robinson, Zurika. 2005. "Corporate Tax Rates in the SADC Region: Determinants and Policy Implications." *South Africa Journal of Economics* 73 (4, December): 722–40.

Russell, Alec. 2007. "South Africa Records the First Fiscal Surplus in Its History." *Financial Times*, February 22, p. 5.

Schiffers, Steve. 2007. "Multinationals Lead India's IT Revolution." BBC News, February 8.

Small Business Project. 2004. "Counting the Cost of Red Tape for Business in South Africa." (http://www.sbp.org.za.)

Steenekamp, T. J. 1996. "Some Aspects of Corporate Taxation in South Africa: The Katz Commission." *South Africa Journal of Economics* 64 (1, March): 1–19.

Stern, Nicholas. 2001. "Investment Climate Assessment." World Bank, Washington, DC, March 22.

STPI (Software Technology Parks of India). 2006. *Annual Report 2006*.

Tucker, Sundeep. 2007. "A Bidding War Makes for 'Crazy' Salaries across Asia." *Financial Times*, May 7, p. 9.

van Blerck, Michael. 1995. "South Africa: Tax Reform of the Katz Commission." *Bulletin for International Fiscal Documentation* 49 (7-8): 360–66.

Van Rensburg, B. P. J. 1990. "Tax Reform Issues in South Africa in the 1990s." *South African Journal of Economics* 58 (1, March): 1–11.

Wilson, Dominic, and Rootha Purushothaman. 2003. *Dreaming with BRICs: The Path to 2050*. Global Economics Paper 99. Goldman Sachs, October (http://www2.goldmansachs.com/insight/research/reports/99.pdf).

World Bank. 2002. *Brazil Jobs Report. Vol. I: Policy Briefing*. Report 24408-BR. Washington, DC: World Bank.

———. 2004. *India: Investment Climate and Manufacturing Industry*. Washington, DC: World Bank, Finance and Private Sector Development Unit, South Asia Region, November (http://www.ifc.org/ifcext/economics.nsf/AttachmentsByTitle/IC-IndiaUpdateDraft.pdf/$FILE/IC-IndiaUpdate-Draft.pdf).

———. 2005a. *India and the Knowledge Economy: Leveraging Strengths and Opportunities*. Washington, DC: World Bank.

————. 2005b. *The Investment Climate Assessment for Brazil*. Washington, DC: World Bank, December (http://www.enterprisesurveys.org/documents/enterprisesurveys/ICA/Brazil_Volume%20I.pdf and http://www.enterprisesurveys.org/documents/enterprisesurveys/ICA/Brazil_Volume%20II.pdf).

————. 2005c. *World Development Report 2005: A Better Investment Climate for Everyone*. Washington, DC: World Bank.

————. 2006a. *Doing Business 2006*. Washington, DC: World Bank (http://www.doingbusiness.org/).

————. 2006b. *Doing Business in South Asia 2006*. Washington, DC: World Bank (http://www-wds.worldbank.org/external/default/WDSContentServer/WDSP/IB/2006/12/20/000020953_20061220103458/Rendered/PDF/369000SAR0Doing0business0200601PUBLIC1.pdf)

————. 2006c. "Sector Study of the Effective Tax Burden: South Africa." Foreign Investment Advisory Service, World Bank Group, Washington, DC, April.

————. 2006d. *Unleashing the Industrial Growth Potential of Uttar Pradesh. India: State-Level Investment Climate Policy Note*. Washington, DC: World Bank, Finance and Private Sector Development Unit, South Asia Region, March.

————. 2007a. *An Assessment of the Investment Climate in South Africa*. Report 3490. Washington, DC: World Bank. (http://siteresources.worldbank.org/EXTAFRSUMAFTPS/Resources/ICA008.pdf).

————. 2007b. *Doing Business 2007: How to Reform*. Washington, DC: World Bank (for an overview, see http://www.doingbusiness.org/documents/DoingBusiness2007_Overview.pdf)

————. 2007c. *Doing Business in Brazil 2007*. Washington, DC: World Bank (http://www.doingbusiness.org/Main/Brazil.aspx and http://www.doingbusiness.org/documents/doing_business_in_brazil_07.pdf).

————. 2007d. *Doing Business in South Asia 2007*. Washington, DC: World Bank. (http://go.worldbank.org/7NFVGMI230).

————. 2007e. *São Paulo: Inputs for a Sustainable Competitive City Strategy*. Washington, DC: World Bank.

World Bank Group Surveys and Other Tools

Doing Business Ranking Simulator. http://www.doingbusiness.org/.

The Investment Climate Survey for Brazil, conducted between July and October 2003 and covering 1,642 manufacturing firms in 13 Brazilian states. http://rrudev.ifc.org/internal/cicic/portal.htm and http://iresearch.worldbank.org/InvestmentClimate/.

The Investment Climate Survey for India, conducted between March and July 2003 and covering 1,860 manufacturing firms sampled from 40 cities in 12 of India's major states; data from the 2006 Investment Climate Survey for India successfully revisited more than half of the firms surveyed in the 2003 survey and further expanded the sample to include more than a dozen new cities and four additional states. http://rrudev.ifc.org/internal/cicic/portal.htm and http://iresearch.worldbank.org/InvestmentClimate/.

The Investment Climate Survey for South Africa, conducted between January and December of 2004 and covering 800 firms, 75 percent of which were in the manufacturing sector, 14 percent in the construction industry, and 11 percent in the wholesale and retail trade. http://rrudev.ifc.org/internal/cicic/portal.htm and http://iresearch.worldbank.org/InvestmentClimate/.